A Teacher's Guide to Managing Autism in the Classroom

Teaching Success From Kindergarten to High School

Richard Bass

Table of Contents

Introduction

Autism is uniqueness and difference personified.
–Amanda J. Friedman

Follow Your Hunch

Miss Wright, a second-grade teacher at a mainstream school, called a parent-teacher meeting with one of the class moms to discuss her son's classroom challenges. For weeks, she had been observing the little boy's behavior, and she suspected that he was living with undiagnosed autism. During playtime, he refused to share his toys and would hit children who attempted to grab them. When reprimanded by the teacher, he would react with explosive emotions.

Group work was another area of concern noted by Miss Wright. She observed that in group settings, the little boy would insist on taking the lead and made his peers do things his way. He also gravitated toward ideas and topics he found interesting and seemed disengaged when the topic changed to something else. The little boy also struggled to follow instructions like eating his food at the lunch table. Instead of abiding by the rules like everyone else, he would go against the grain and eat his lunch on the floor.

The parent was aware of her son's social and communication challenges, but rejected the suspicion that he might have autism. "My son is one of the brightest students in your class," she petitioned. "I know he lacks concentration and acts silly sometimes, but isn't that a normal stage of development?"

The parent did have a point. Her son was academically superior to other students in the class and could complete math sums at a fourth-grade level. However, his intelligence didn't rule him out for autism, especially because autistic children often tend to be gifted in a particular area.

Miss Wright managed to convince the parent to seek a professional opinion from a child specialist. The results from the initial assessment showed that he indeed displayed symptoms of autism spectrum disorder (ASD), and so, he underwent a full assessment to diagnose and provide the most suitable treatment for his condition.

Did you know that teachers are often the first to notice the symptoms of autism in children before their parents intervene? Perhaps the reason for this is that classroom environments are structured and predictable, which makes it easier to detect behaviors that are outside the norm. It isn't farfetched to believe that there could be some students in your classroom who are on the spectrum but have yet to be diagnosed. This is particularly why you need to gain a deeper understanding of

ASD and the various ways it manifests—so that you can initiate the process of getting students the support they deserve.

The Purpose of This Book

All students have the right to quality education. However, accessing quality education is a struggle for students with learning and developmental disabilities. ASD symptoms like impulsivity, inattention, inappropriate social interactions, and sensory issues create learning barriers for students in the classroom. If they get too overwhelmed by their symptoms, they might withdraw or display challenging behaviors.

Your patience and encouragement go a long way toward helping students with ASD keep up with the pace of learning and enjoy coming to school. The purpose of this book is to show you several ways to provide academic and social support for students who may be exhibiting signs of autism. You will be presented with modern and evidence-based strategies that can enhance the learning environment of all your students.

There is a wealth of information to learn in this guide, whether you are new to teaching or have been teaching for several years. You will gain a deeper understanding of autism spectrum disorder and have access to the latest research, learning models, and instruction strategies to support diverse student needs, promote academic success, and create an inclusive classroom environment.

The Structure of the Book

For added convenience, this comprehensive guide has been broken down into four parts. Each part explores and discusses a theme related to managing ASD behaviors in the classroom. Here is an overview of the four parts.

Part 1: Understanding ASD and Your Role as an Educator

Key questions:

- What are the characteristics of ASD?

- What signs and symptoms should I be looking for?

- What professional help can I offer students with ASD?

- How can I work with parents and doctors to support my students?

Part 2: Managing ASD-Related Behaviors in the Classroom

Key questions:

- What are some unique learning challenges that students with ASD experience?

- How can I adjust my instructions and materials to create an inclusive learning experience?

- What are some ASD-friendly ways of managing classroom behaviors and addressing sensory sensitivities?

Part 3: ASD-Friendly Communication in the Classroom

Key questions:

- How can I promote positive and collaborative social interactions between students with ASD and their peers in class?

- Are there any strategies to help students who struggle with language and literacy skills?

- What can I do to teach my students how to manage time wisely and work independently?

Part 4: Supportive Classroom Strategies for Students at All Levels

Key question:

- Can you provide specific solutions for students at the elementary, middle school, and high school levels?

At the end of each chapter (applicable for Parts 1–3) are group and individual activities that you can practice with other educators or alone. These activities are designed to help you engage with the content and utilize the skills learned throughout the chapters in real-time.

Prepare to explore the minds of students with ASD like you have never done before. This guide will present you with all the necessary information you need to know to provide them with a comfortable and supportive learning experience. Without further ado, let's get started with the master class!

PART 1:

Understanding ASD and Your Role as an Educator

Chapter 1:

Understanding Autism Spectrum Disorder (ASD)

Autism is not a processing error. It's a different operating system.
–Sarah Hendrickx

Defining ASD

Autism spectrum disorder (ASD) is a developmental condition that causes several cognitive and behavioral challenges due to brain impairments and may also affect the ability to read, write, talk, and memorize information. (Centers for Disease Control and Prevention, n.d.-b).

Children diagnosed with ASD can be referred to as either "autistic children" or "children with autism," depending on individual preferences. Studies have shown that 87% of adults diagnosed with autism prefer identity-first language (i.e., "autistic adult"), but professionals and the friends and family of persons diagnosed with autism prefer to use person-first language (i.e., "adult with autism") (Diament, 2022). In this book, we have chosen to use identity-first language, as this is how autistic students would likely prefer to be addressed.

When doctors diagnose ASD, they don't take blood samples or conduct medical tests like other childhood disorders. Instead, they will seek to learn more about the patient's developmental history and behavioral issues to make a diagnosis. Signs of ASD can be detected from as young as 18 months and a full assessment can be administered by the age of two. Nevertheless, a late diagnosis of ASD is not uncommon, since for many children, these early signs can be missed.

Since children do not reach developmental milestones all at the same time, parents, doctors, and teachers commonly misinterpret ASD symptoms as normal developmental delays. Moreover, some children with ASD do not display behaviors that are different from their peers. For instance, they might be average or above average academically, may display good social skills, and might show no signs of challenging behavior. These children are known to have low support needs because of their ability to mask their ASD symptoms and appear to be the same as everyone else. It is only when the disorder progresses or when children are presented with highly stressful or traumatic life circumstances that their symptoms are unmasked.

Identifying ASD in the classroom environment can be difficult because not every student with the condition will behave poorly. In general, students with ASD are known to be gifted in particular areas like sports, creativity, or academics. Their above-average performance in these areas allows them to fly under the radar and go through school without being suspected of living with a developmental condition. Other areas of giftedness include social interactions and communication. Some naturally sociable students may not have trouble making friends or recognizing social cues. However, as students progress to higher grades and classwork becomes more strenuous, they may start to showcase classic signs of ASD such as losing focus, fidgeting, obsessive and impulsive behaviors, or feeling social anxiety in specific classroom contexts.

Another trigger that might exacerbate ASD symptoms is sensory overload. Sensory processing issues are one of the common signs of ASD. They occur when students are overstimulated to the point of feeling overwhelmed. Some of the classroom experiences that can cause sensory overload include dim or bright lights, loud noises, crowded classrooms or hallways, hot or cold temperatures, cluttered desks, and unpleasant smells. Outbursts and meltdowns that are triggered by sensory overload can be mistaken as difficult behavior when the source of the triggers is unknown.

Diagnosing ASD

The length of time between first discovering ASD symptoms and getting the proper treatment for it can span from several months to a year. During that time, children can be referred to various specialists who make their observations and rule out the possibility of co-occurring disorders like anxiety, attention-deficit hyperactivity disorder (ADHD), post-traumatic stress disorder (PTSD), and obsessive-compulsive disorder (OCD).

Very young children might go through a stage of developmental monitoring where they are observed by doctors on an ongoing basis to see whether they are reaching important developmental milestones that they need to reach at various ages. Parents and teachers can participate in developmental monitoring by keeping track of children's behaviors at home and school and taking note of sudden changes. Tools like the developmental milestone checklist or the CDC Milestone Tracker app are great ways to assess whether children are meeting their milestones.

The diagnostic process begins with a routine screening administered by a family doctor, which can take the form of a checklist or questionnaire. This is a more formalized approach to developmental monitoring that can lead to children being referred to specialists if there are any concerns found. The type of specialists children are referred to can be pediatricians, child psychologists, speech-language pathologists, or occupational therapists. These specialists will perform an in-depth developmental evaluation that might include observations, structured tests, interviews with parents, and completing questionnaires.

The results of the in-depth evaluation will determine whether the diagnostic criteria for ASD have been met. Several conditions have been placed under the umbrella of ASD, such as autistic disorder, Asperger's syndrome, and pervasive developmental disorder not otherwise specified (PDD-NOS). Doctors use the American Psychiatric Association's handbook, commonly known as the *Diagnostic and Statistical Manual of Mental Disorders (DSM)*, to diagnose and treat a range of mental health disorders, including ASD.

The most current edition of the DSM, the DSM-5, provides guidelines on how to diagnose ASD. For starters, children must display three out of three listed challenges in social interactions and communication, which include (Children's Hospital of Philadelphia, 2020):

- challenges with social-emotional reciprocity such as initiating conversations, facilitating back-and-forth conversations, and expressing or understanding emotions.

- challenges with displaying and understanding normal nonverbal communication. This might include avoiding eye contact, displaying abnormal body language, and having trouble picking up on social cues or interpreting other people's body language.

- challenges in building and maintaining relationships with other people apart from their caregivers. This might also include a lack of interest in social interactions or difficulty in responding with appropriate behaviors in different social contexts.

Furthermore, children must meet at least two out of four of the following symptoms related to repetitive and restrictive interests, activities, and behaviors:

- repeating certain words or phrases (including inappropriate phrases learned from television or other people)

- an adherence to a rigid routine or demonstrating ritualized patterns of verbal or nonverbal behavior, which is often accompanied by an extreme resistance to change

- having a strong attachment or obsession with very specific objects, topics, or interests. These can include unusual fascinations like observing bus schedules.

- high or low reactivity to sensory stimuli, such as a strong dislike of certain smells or fabrics. Children may also demonstrate an unusual interest in specific sensory inputs, such as a fascination with lights, sounds, textures, or smells.

When diagnosing patients, doctors are urged to rule out developmental delays and co-occurring conditions. The criteria are also based on current and past functioning, which means that older children who may have not shown signs of ASD in their early childhood years can still be diagnosed with ASD in their adolescence.

Spend some time familiarizing yourself with the DSM-5 diagnostic criteria for ASD to understand the various ways in which the condition can affect students. Throughout the book, we will be addressing these symptoms in more detail and looking at evidence-based strategies that can help you manage them in the classroom environment.

Understanding the Autism Spectrum

You may have heard the phrase "on the spectrum" being used when referring to autism. The phrase refers to the diverse ways in which ASD can present itself. For example, we know that there are several sets of behavioral and developmental challenges that students with ASD can experience. However, not everyone will experience the same symptoms, nor will their symptoms be at the same severity. Since autism affects students differently, we refer to them as being on the spectrum.

Another reason why autism is known as a spectrum disorder is due to the five subtypes that it includes. Students who are diagnosed with ASD could be living with one of the following conditions.

Autistic Disorder

Autistic disorder is commonly known as the "classic" type of autism. For many years, this was the only recognized presentation of autism. It is characterized by social and communication challenges, as well as repetitive and restrictive behaviors.

Asperger's Syndrome

Before 2013, Asperger's syndrome used to be classified as a standalone disorder. Today, it is included under the ASD umbrella and regarded as a subtype of autism. Some of the unique characteristics of this disorder include impressive cognitive strengths such as strong working memory or problem-solving abilities. Unlike patients with autistic disorder, those with Asperger's syndrome show no signs of language or cognitive delays, but will however display other classic symptoms of autism such as inattention or a lack of impulse control.

Pervasive Developmental Disorder Not Otherwise Specified (PDD-NOS)

Doctors have discovered that patients diagnosed with PDD-NOS fall between autistic disorder and Asperger's syndrome. In comparison with the two other subtypes, patients with PDD-NOS display severe symptoms of Asperger's syndrome, but not enough to classify them with autistic disorder. Doctors use this subtype to group children with unusual presentations of autism that don't neatly fit into other subtypes.

Childhood Disintegrative Disorder

Childhood disintegrative disorder, also referred to as Heller's syndrome and disintegrative psychosis, is the rarest type of autism. It is diagnosed in patients who go through the normal stages of development in the first two to three years, then experience a dramatic cognitive regression that causes them to lose their acquired skills and develop a developmental disorder such as autism.

Rett Syndrome

Rett syndrome is a rare neurological disorder that primarily affects little girls. It causes brain development impairments and leads to cognitive and developmental disabilities. Some of the symptoms of Rett syndrome include lack of eye contact, social withdrawal, and communication challenges, which are similar to classic autism. In the DSM-4, Rett was included as a subtype of ASD because of its features; however, when doctors discovered that it is caused by genetics, it was given its distinct classification.

As you can see, there are many ways that autism can present itself. Children who don't necessarily fit under specific labels but display some of the main characteristics of autism can be accommodated and receive the appropriate treatment. Doctors are also aware that close to three-quarters of all autistic children are diagnosed with co-occurring psychiatric conditions (Conditions That Can Occur With Autism, 2022). These conditions can be dormant or active at any time during children's development. Some of the common co-occurring psychiatric conditions include

- generalized anxiety disorder

- attention-deficit hyperactivity disorder (ADHD)

- bipolar disorder

- clinical depression

- Down syndrome

- eating disorders

- sleep problems

- motor difficulties

- Tourette syndrome

- tuberous sclerosis

- fragile X syndrome

- seizures and epilepsy

- gastrointestinal problems

- obsessive-compulsive disorder

- speech and language disorders

- intellectual disability and developmental delays

These conditions require separate diagnoses alongside the ASD diagnosis. Doctors may also prescribe medications and various therapy options to manage the symptoms.

How Does ASD Impact Learning and Social Interactions?

We have taken an in-depth look into ASD and how the disorder is diagnosed. However, what we haven't fully unpacked is how ASD affects students' learning outcomes.

There are some important things to note when teaching students with ASD.

The first is that students with ASD won't exhibit identical symptoms. Remember, autism is a spectrum disorder that can be presented in multiple ways. Secondly, students with ASD are likely to experience developmental delays, which means that they may not develop skills at the same pace as their classmates. Some students may need additional support to remember or carry out certain instructions. Identifying the student's strengths and leveraging special interests can enhance their ability to focus and memorize information.

Moreover, students with ASD have a unique way of socializing. Sometimes their behaviors could be considered inappropriate because they don't correspond with standard acceptable behaviors. Learning more about these social and communication challenges and reinforcing desirable behaviors will promote healthier student–teacher and peer relationships.

In addition to this, students with ASD may experience processing challenges such as difficulty processing information or sensory inputs. For instance, they may struggle to learn new material, organize their thoughts, manage their time effectively, or recall information. Sensory sensitivities such as the sensitivity to light or noise could cause frequent interruptions to their learning experience, making it difficult to stay focused and complete classwork.

Lastly, a significant factor that affects students' ability to follow in class is the prevalence of anxiety. It is common for students on the spectrum to develop some type of anxiety disorder, such as specific phobias, social anxiety, or panic disorder. Classroom anxiety can be triggered by several factors, including going through transitions, fear of failure, bullying, lack of comprehension, fear or avoidance of objects, and time pressures. The presence of anxiety makes it harder for students to concentrate on tasks, form positive relationships with peers, or stay organized and on track with work.

Bear in mind that ASD is not a learning disability; however, due to cognitive impairments and processing issues, students with ASD can struggle with learning at school—some may even get diagnosed with co-occurring learning disabilities like dyslexia, speech and language disorders, or ADHD, which directly impact a student's ability to learn. Nevertheless, with the right teaching approach and a supportive environment, students can thrive academically and build successful social lives inside and outside of the classroom.

Group Activity: Reflect on Your Experiences With ASD

Sit around a table with other educators and take turns sharing your experiences interacting with students who were diagnosed or showed symptoms of ASD. Describe the early warning signs you observed that may be core characteristics of ASD. Explain what actions you took to provide support, such as contacting the parents or seeking a second opinion from another teacher.

Individual Activity: Learn More About ASD

ASD is a wide and varied disorder that can be studied at length. Take some time to deepen your knowledge and understanding of ASD by reading more on this topic. Visit the following blogs and websites to access more information about ASD and how you can support affected students:

- Autism Spectrum Teacher (autismspectrumteacher.com/blog)

- Autism Classroom (autismclassroom.com/blog-posts)

- Autism Little Learners (autismlittlelearners.com/blog)

- Autism Classroom Resources (autismclassroomresources.com/blog/)

- Autism Awareness Centre Inc (autismawarenesscentre.com)

In this chapter, you have learned what ASD is, how it is diagnosed, and the various ways it can impact the learning experiences of students. We will now proceed to the next chapter and discuss your unique role as a teacher in supporting students with ASD.

Chapter 2:

The Educator's Role in Supporting Students with ASD

Autism doesn't come with an instruction guide. It comes with a family who will never give up.
–Kerry Magro

The Value of Creating an Inclusive Classroom Culture

Imagine standing in front of your classroom and looking at the diversity of students representing different races, genders, ethnic groups, cultures, religions, and disabilities. You can see native English-speaking students and others who are multilingual; introverted students and others who bring entertainment to the class; neurotypical students and others who are neurodivergent. All of these students, despite their diverse backgrounds and unique challenges, are engaged and following as you deliver instructions. They are all on the same page and feel accommodated by your inclusive teaching approach.

Inclusivity is one of the buzzwords of this modern age. It refers to recognizing and embracing differences, viewing them as assets rather than liabilities. It is becoming less common to find homogenous classroom environments where everybody looks and thinks the same. Nowadays, classrooms represent cultures from across the world and are made up of students with different learning needs. Mainstream schools accept both neurotypical and neurodivergent students and provide free and equal access to education.

At the heart of inclusivity is recognizing that every student possesses unique abilities that can positively contribute to the success of the whole classroom when they are nurtured. This means that differences among students are not deficits but, rather, potential strengths. Students with ASD may be above average compared to their peers when it comes to reading, writing, and mathematical skills, but may come up short in other tasks like staying organized, regulating emotions, and participating in classroom discussions. Your challenge as a teacher is to create opportunities for all students to demonstrate their strengths while providing adequate support for their shortcomings.

Throughout the book, you will be taken through teaching practices that promote inclusivity—meaning, they accommodate students from all walks of life. These practices can be incorporated into your lesson plans to provide a supportive learning experience. No student will feel confused or left behind, because these practices cater to a diverse range of learning styles.

Creating an inclusive classroom begins with a mindset shift. Two important skills that you will need to develop and practice to make this shift are showing empathy and being flexible.

Empathetic Teaching Environment

Empathy is the ability to step inside someone else's shoes and experience reality from their perspective. An empathetic teaching environment seeks to understand students' learning needs and provide the necessary support to make the experience more enjoyable. As an educator, you can create this type of environment by doing the following:

- **Building positive student–teacher relationships:** Establish personal connections with students so that you can learn about their strengths, interests, and areas of concern. This can be done through regular one-on-one check-ins, classroom discussions, or personalized feedback on assignments.

- **Providing positive reinforcement:** Pay attention to what students are good at and offer praise to keep them motivated. Encourage the behavior you desire to see more of, rather than putting a spotlight on challenging behaviors. Students will feel confident in themselves, and this will reflect positively in their classwork and classroom behaviors.

- **Understanding various triggers:** There might be certain classroom rules, objects, or transitions that trigger stress or anxiety for students. Find out what those experiences are through ongoing observations and discussions with students and make the necessary adjustments or replacements to limit students' exposure to triggers.

Flexible Teaching Environment

Being flexible means having the ability to willingly modify your methods for better outcomes. When teaching a diverse group of students, it is important to remain flexible in your teaching approach to accommodate various learning needs and styles. Some of the ways to create a flexible teaching environment include:

- **Providing access to various learning materials:** Find creative and diverse ways to present information to students, taking into consideration their learning challenges as well as special interests and preferred learning formats (e.g., verbal instruction, video, demonstrations, etc.).

- **Finding engaging ways to give instructions:** Not every student responds well to direct instructions. Explore alternative instructional methods that can drive engagement, such as asking questions, creating group tasks, or presenting stories and case studies.

- **Offering options when creating assignments:** Provide students with a choice on how they can submit their assignments. This allows students to choose their preferred learning method. For instance, some students might opt for a written submission while others may enjoy creating video submissions or conducting experiments.

Showing empathy and adopting flexible teaching methods is a great start to cultivating an inclusive classroom environment. However, all of this effort must be founded on positive relationships with your students.

Building Positive Relationships With Students With ASD

In the previous chapter, we looked at the impact of ASD symptoms on students' classroom experience. One of the symptoms mentioned was the prevalence of anxiety. Students with ASD are likely to suffer from anxiety due to their learning disabilities and developmental delays. These differences become more visible as students reach higher grades and notice that they do not respond to situations like their peers. Some may even get into the habit of skipping school or socially withdrawing from others as a result of their anxiety.

Building a strong relationship with your students, including those with ASD, enables you to understand their needs and provide access to support when they need it. Through casual and respectful one-on-one conversations, you can learn about your students' learning struggles, family backgrounds, and peer relationships. It is also the case that students who feel valued are more likely to feel comfortable participating in class or asking for help compared to students who feel sidelined. Some may even be motivated to work harder because of the amount of respect they have for you.

The best time to start building relationships with your students is the first day of the school year; otherwise, you can catch up by starting immediately. Something else worth mentioning is that these relationships require ongoing maintenance. For instance, if you are going to start a habit of scheduling one-on-one performance feedback sessions with your students, remain consistent throughout the year. Communication doesn't need to be frequent; however, it must be consistent. Decide how regularly you want to facilitate group and individual interactions with your students and stick to the schedule.

A great way to build positive relationships is to create classroom rituals that promote friendly and respectful exchanges with your students. Below are some suggestions that you are welcome to modify and implement with your students:

- Greet your students when they enter the classroom and say goodbye when they leave. Make the exchange of pleasantries fun so that children are motivated to participate.

- During classroom discussions, ask students to raise their hands to answer questions and allow different students the opportunity to speak.

- Create assignments that allow students to express their interests, hobbies, and talents. Keep a record of this information and design lessons centered around students' varied interests, hobbies, and talents.

- Offer public praise and recognition to students who are making progress or have shown recent improvements. Create a rewards chart or system to keep track of students' accomplishments.

- Identify the student of the month—this could be someone who has exhibited respect and kindness toward others. Announce the recipient publicly and put their face or name on the classroom wall. Choose different students each month until all students have received the honor.

- Schedule parent–teacher meetings once a term and invite students to join. Share students' achievements with parents and create unique goals that students can focus on.

- Give students a say on how lessons are designed or what rules and norms are followed in the classroom. This creates a sense of ownership and belonging, leading to higher engagement.

- Be approachable and have moments where you let your guard down. Students need to find you relatable to strengthen trust, so share your interests, talk about your pets, and connect on things that make you laugh to lighten the atmosphere in the classroom.

Collaborating With Parents and Support Professionals

Supporting students with ASD isn't something that you do alone. Since this is a medical disorder that affects various aspects of students' lives, it is crucial to collaborate with parents and professionals like doctors or psychologists to provide the necessary support. To work as a TEAM carries the following meaning:

- Together

- Everyone

- Achieves

- More

There is certain information that you won't know or have access to, just as parents and doctors may not be aware of certain information that you have observed and recorded. Regularly meeting with parents and support staff (if necessary) enables you to exchange notes, establish suitable learning goals and outcomes, as well as plan and monitor interventions. Of course, students, especially those in higher grades, should never be left out of these discussions since they have the right to make their own choices.

There is a difference between advocating for students with ASD and collaborating with parents to provide a meaningful learning experience for students with ASD. Advocacy means defending the rights of students, such as making referrals to your school district to get students placed inside certain schools or enrolled in special education programs. While this is an important role to play as an educator, it doesn't require you to form partnerships with parents and support staff.

Collaboration is student-centered and based on making wise decisions about students' educational future. Certain issues are brought up to allow for open discussions around possible solutions and interventions.

There are three crucial components to creating successful collaborations, which we will go into below.

Provide Students With a Voice

Collaboration cannot exist without the participation of students. The level of participation will vary depending on how old students are. Young students may not have the ability to express their needs or concerns as articulately as older students. Thus, their level of participation will be minimal compared to older students. Providing students a voice begins in the classroom with the opportunities they are given to communicate their needs, offer feedback, and set meaningful academic goals. Younger students can be taught how to make choices by being presented with options. For instance, they can choose which writing tools to work with or how instructions are given to them.

Build Healthy Relationships With Parents

Introduce yourself to parents and provide various communication channels that they can use to get in touch with you. Establish regular correspondence through newsletters, announcements, parent–teacher meetings, or student performance feedback sessions. The foundation of a healthy parent–teacher relationship is trust and openness. Therefore, don't withhold concerns you may have about their children.

Be mindful of how they might receive negative feedback—they might remain in denial or respond with fear. Many times, parents are unaware of underlying learning or developmental disabilities their children may have, while others may be overstretched at home and may not have the appropriate resources to seek help. Reassure parents that your role is to ensure that their children get the support they need, even if it means referring them to professionals who could offer more specialized assistance.

Strengthen Home–School Learning

To help students with ASD develop certain skills, training must be carried out in the classroom and reinforced at home. It isn't enough to expose students to skills in a classroom setting only, as they need ongoing practice to learn them.

Work together with parents to create a learning environment at home. Give them tips on setting up a workstation or a designated room for schoolwork, organizing books and school documents in storage folders, and establishing structured and predictable study and homework routines. If there are specific projects that require parents' involvement, give them notice ahead of time so they can schedule time and prepare the necessary materials. If you are going to send daily behavior reports home, ask parents to read and sign the reports and return them to you.

It takes a village to raise and teach students with ASD, and everybody's role, whether small or large, is significant to students' growth and educational success. When they realize how much support they have around them, they feel encouraged to do their best at school and let their strengths shine!

Group Activity: Host a Panel Discussion

Host a panel discussion at school and invite guest speakers such as school teachers, parents of students with ASD, members of your school district, and child doctors specializing in diagnosing or treating ASD. The theme of the panel discussion should be related to promoting a culture of inclusivity in the classroom. Encourage dialogue around the learning experiences of students with disabilities and collaborate on finding solutions.

Individual Activity: Reflect on the Inclusivity in Your Classroom

Reflect on your current teaching practices and consider how inclusive they are of students with ASD. Read over the symptoms mentioned in Chapter 1 and determine whether your instructions, learning materials, and lesson structures are flexible enough to accommodate your students. You can also reflect on the quality of your relationships with students and identify rituals that you can adopt to improve communication.

In this chapter, we have explored the importance of creating an inclusive classroom environment for the empowerment of all students. We can now proceed to the next chapter and discuss the significance and step-by-step process of carrying out individualized education plans (IEPs).

Chapter 3:

Individualized Education Plans (IEPs) and Differentiated Instruction

Life is 10% what happens to you and 90% how you react to it.
–Charles R. Swindoll

What Is the Purpose of an Individualized Education Plan?

The U.S. Department of Education has arrangements put in place to provide additional support to students with disabilities. The specific law that legalizes special education services is called the Individuals with Disabilities Education Act (IDEA). The IDEA protects the rights of students with disabilities and ensures that they receive equal access to and opportunities for quality education. It applies to students who are in state, public, charter, and some private schools. It also facilitates the enrollment of students with disabilities into special education programs.

When supporting students with disabilities, school districts must provide access to free public education. Both neurotypical and neurodivergent students must learn side-by-side, completing the same curriculum as much as possible. When certain learning disabilities are identified in students, schools are required to schedule a free evaluation at no cost to the families. The evaluation determines whether students are suffering from any medical conditions and how severe their challenges may be. Students who qualify for special education services will be taken through a structured and comprehensive individualized education plan (IEP) to create intervention goals and objectives and to identify appropriate services.

Before you can enroll your students for the IEP, there is a process that you and their parents need to go through to assess whether they qualify for this program. Not all students with learning disabilities (or symptoms of learning disabilities) will meet the requirements for an IEP. For instance, one of the qualifying criteria is that students' disabilities need to be severe to the extent of interfering with their ability to function in the classroom. As the teacher, you can use your notes and reports to highlight the reason why you have identified some students as needing to be placed on special education services. These documents will be evaluated alongside medical assessments from child specialists.

A committee of professionals, including members of the school district and child doctors, will go through the evaluation and either approve or reject students for the special education program. Parents are welcome to contest rulings if they are unsatisfied with the outcomes. Qualifying students will proceed to the next step, which is the IEP meeting.

Parents and teachers will meet with the committee to discuss the student's school performance, their strengths and weaknesses, and any specific learning challenges they may have. The team will also discuss recommendations, intervention goals and objectives, and special services to offer students.

According to the IDEA, IEPs must be reviewed annually to ensure that students are reaching targeted milestones and that the services offered are helping to improve their performance at school. During the review phase, modifications can be made to IEPs if necessary.

Writing and Implementing IEPs for Students with ASD

Students with ASD may struggle to keep up with their neurotypical peers in the classroom due to cognitive and behavioral challenges. Having carefully designed IEPs outlines specific goals and objectives that students can focus on to catch up to their classmates socially, behaviorally, and academically.

Below is the step-by-step process on how you would implement an IEP.

Step 1: Define the Learning Team

The first step is to identify members of the learning team. These should be individuals who will work together to provide support to the student and their family. A standard learning team consists of the student, classroom teacher, special education teacher, parents or guardians, and child specialists such as social workers, psychologists, or occupational therapists. The participation of young students below the age of 10 is not necessary unless they are interested and would like to be included.

Step 2: Present the Strengths and Academic Needs

Once you have formed the learning team, decide on a date and time when you can meet to discuss the IEP. Go through the evaluation summary and highlight key strengths and weaknesses that have been identified. Clarify information that may be difficult for the student or parents to understand. You may also need to explain the specific academic needs that the student has, and how those needs impact their learning. Specialists may be able to explain how ASD symptoms affect the student's performance and behaviors and what areas they need to work on moving forward.

Step 3: Set Goals

Create intervention goals and objectives together. Each goal should seek to address an academic need. This means that if there are five academic needs identified, there must be five goals written down. If the student has an existing IEP from the previous year, read over the goals and update them to ensure they are addressing current needs and challenges. Goals should follow the SMART goal-setting framework (the next section will go into detail on how you can structure goals).

Step 4: Understand the Accommodations and Modifications

The IEP includes sections for specific accommodations and modifications that the student is eligible for. As a team, you can decide what those accommodations and modifications will be. Accommodations are adjustments to the expectations that students are required to follow to enable them to showcase their skills and knowledge without lowering the academic standard or changing the learning outcomes. In contrast, modifications provide a completely new set of expectations students are required to follow, which cause content changes that may or may not lower the grade-level standard. There are some cases where modifications are beneficial. For example, a student who has a meltdown whenever they are given writing tasks or required to use writing tools may be given assignments through technological devices like tablets or given access to speech-to-text software.

Step 5: Ensure IEP Success

After you have written the IEP, monitor the student's progress and be responsive to any adjustments that are needed. Continue to meet with the learning team to exchange information and review the IEP. You can decide how often to review the IEP—whether it may be quarterly or annually. During reviews, assess the effectiveness of the interventions and support provided. Get feedback from the student to hear what is working well and what needs to be improved.

How to Set Effective IEP Goals Using the SMART Goal-Setting Technique

Establishing effective IEP goals is so important that it needs a section of its own. IEP goals play a valuable role in managing ASD symptoms, addressing academic needs, and bringing out the strengths of students with ASD. They create a clear and realistic road map that students and teachers can follow to work on core deficits and track progress along the way.

The SMART goal-setting technique is a framework that is used to structure goals. The popular goal-setting acronym, SMART, is short for specific, measurable, achievable, relevant, and time-bound, and these should be the five criteria you use to plan goals. IEP goals need to meet these five criteria for them to be monitored and evaluated. Below is a brief overview of the framework:

- **Specific:** Goals should be clearly defined in one or two sentences and must consist of a single desired outcome.

- **Measurable:** Specific quantitative or qualitative metrics should be included to track progress and milestones.

- **Achievable:** Goals need to be designed with the student's strengths and weaknesses, characteristics, and abilities in mind.

- **Relevant:** Goals should address the specific learning and developmental needs identified in the evaluation report.

- **Time-bound:** Realistic timeframes must be set to create a sense of urgency and help teachers set weekly, monthly, or quarterly objectives.

There are four crucial skills to address when creating IEP goals for students with ASD. Students may not lack all of these skills; however, addressing them can boost their overall performance and success in the classroom. The following is a breakdown of each skill along with a few examples of goals that you can establish for students.

Social and Communication Skills

Social and communication skills are essential for positive student–teacher and peer relationships. Students who are good communicators may also feel confident asking questions and seeking help. Below are goals you can set to help students improve their social and communication skills:

Goals	Objectives
Conversation skills	Teach students how to take turns, engage in back-and-forth conversations, and ask the right questions.
Nonverbal communication skills	Teach students how to communicate through facial expressions, gestures, and sign language to convey their thoughts and feelings.
Social cue awareness	Teach students how to recognize and respond appropriately to social cues such as the changes to one's tone of voice, body language, or facial expressions.
Perspective-taking	Teach students how to

Goals	Objectives
	empathize with others and take on different perspectives during discussions.
Collaboration and cooperation with peers and teachers	Teach students how to work in groups, share responsibilities with team members, solve problems with peers, and follow instructions given by the educator.

Academic Skills

Even though ASD is not classified as a learning disability, students with ASD can experience academic challenges that affect their ability to read, write, memorize information, or solve problems. The goals below can address various academic needs and improve students' overall learning experience.

Goals	Objectives
Executive functioning skills	Teach students how to follow routines, organize their tasks, manage time effectively, and follow instructions when completing tasks.
Critical thinking skills	Teach students how to analyze information, make connections between separate pieces of information, and come up with logical conclusions.
Expressive language skills	Teach students how to verbalize their thoughts and emotions using

Goals	Objectives
	appropriate vocabulary and grammar.
Receptive language skills	Teach students how to understand spoken language, follow directions, interpret written instructions, and engage in classroom discussions.
Visual support	Provide visual aids such as charts and schedules to enhance memory recall and understanding.

Independence and Life Skills

Students with ASD tend to struggle with managing transitions and working independently. By helping them develop independence and learn important life skills, you can empower them to take ownership of their school performance and future academic success. Here are some goals that you can set to cultivate these skills:

Goals	Objectives
Time management	Teach students how to follow schedules, prioritize tasks, create study timetables, and transition between activities without assistance.
Organizational skills	Teach students how to keep their desks tidy, organize their belongings, and make use of storage facilities.

Goals	Objectives
Decision-making skills	Provide students with options and teach them how to make the right choices, consider the consequences of their behaviors, and follow through with their decisions by taking action.
Self-awareness	Teach students how to recognize their strengths and weaknesses, regulate their emotions, set healthy boundaries with others, and advocate for their needs.
College and employment readiness skills	Help students prepare for postsecondary education or employment by setting goals, developing skills necessary for college or employment, conducting research, and identifying their interests and passions.

Behavior and Emotional Regulation Skills

Students with ASD can at times have difficulty regulating their emotions, especially when they experience social anxiety or feel overwhelmed with sensory overload. To avoid meltdowns and other challenging behaviors in the classroom, you can set goals to reinforce healthy coping behaviors, such as:

Goals	Objectives
Self-regulation skills	Teach students how to identify, process, and independently manage

Goals	Objectives
	strong emotions without acting on them.
Focus and attention	Enhance students' concentration in the classroom by modifying teaching practices, incorporating special interests, and providing incentives for staying focused.
Stress-management skills	Teach students positive coping skills to manage stress and anxiety, such as how to self-soothe, take deep breaths, or handle sensory overload.
Conflict resolution skills	Teach students how to resolve conflict peacefully through effective problem-solving and communication strategies.
Flexibility	Teach students how to adapt to new expectations in class or deal with sudden changes to their routine by developing flexible thinking.

Group Activity: Mock IEP Meeting Roleplay

Come together with other teachers and conduct a mock IEP meeting. Assign each teacher a role to play in the meeting and discuss the evaluation report of a hypothetical student with ASD who has been approved for special education services. Go through the steps of developing the IEP, then afterward, reflect on the process and seek clarity on steps that you don't understand.

Individual Activity: Create SMART Goals

Identify a student in your class who has demonstrated certain academic or behavioral challenges. Focus on a specific skill they seem to be lacking and establish a SMART goal to support them. Note that the student doesn't need to be on the spectrum. The purpose of this activity is to practice creating SMART goals that address core learning needs.

In this chapter, you have learned the value of special education services for students with ASD. You have also been guided through the process of developing effective IEPs to address academic and social needs.

We have now completed the first part of the book, which focuses on understanding ASD and your role as an educator. We can now proceed to the second part of the book and consider evidence-based strategies for managing ASD-related behaviors in the classroom.

PART 2:

Managing ASD-Related Behaviors in the Classroom

Chapter 4:

Understanding and Addressing Sensory Sensitivities

Sometimes the things that make us different are the things that make us strong.
–Unknown

Recognizing Common Sensory Sensitivities in Students With ASD

A common issue that students with ASD encounter is sensory overload. This occurs whenever students are overwhelmed by a range of sensory stimuli or when they experience a sensation that they dislike. Scientists have done experiments to investigate the relationship between sensory overload and ASD. They have discovered that people with ASD cannot process large amounts of sensory input at a time (Davis, 2021). The best way to describe it would be attempting to watch 10 TV shows at the same time and trying to follow the storylines of each one. You would feel confused, frustrated, and increasingly stressed trying to process all of that information at once.

Neurotypical students can block out some sensory inputs and direct their focus to specific ones. For instance, the sound of classmates talking softly in the background wouldn't be distracting for most neurotypical students. However, the same cannot be said for students with ASD, who don't have control over which sensations to ignore and which ones to pay attention to. Their brains pick up on every small and large, soft and loud, dim and bright sensory input. Not only would they be distracted by classmates chatting in the background, but the noise may ring very loud in their ears and sound as though their classmates were yelling, even though the other students have been talking softly.

How students with ASD experience sensory overload will vary depending on their particular sensory processing issue. They may either be hypersensitive or hyposensitive to sensory stimuli. Hypersensitivity refers to overreacting to the sensations in the environment. The student may find everything from the grip of the pencil to the smell of the air freshener intensified and overwhelming. On the other hand, hyposensitivity refers to showing little to no reactions to the sensations in the environment. For instance, the student may have trouble following instructions because they can't hear or understand what the teacher is saying.

Hypersensitive students get easily triggered by busy, cluttered, or chaotic environments. To calm themselves down, some might zone out and daydream or do what is known as stimming, which refers to repetitive behaviors like nail-biting or rocking the body that allows people with ASD to calm down and cope with stressful emotions.

Hyposensitive students have different sensory problems. They have an underreaction to sensory input, meaning that they need more sensory input than normal to feel something. They like noisy areas, touching different objects, chewing inedible objects, and smelling a wide range of scents (some students may be fascinated by strange scents). They also have an abundance of energy and may choose to run when they can simply walk, play-fight with other children, or hug and embrace people. They are prone to falling, crashing into walls, and invading other people's personal space.

Another symptom of hyposensitivity is the inability to feel pain or warmth. Students may unintentionally injure themselves while walking or running and only realize it later. Various safety precautions can be taken in the classroom to prevent injuries, such as implementing a no-running rule, having clear and uncluttered pathways, and keeping sharp objects like scissors away from young students.

There are a range of therapies that can help students manage their sensory processing issues. Some of the common ones include speech therapy to assist with swallowing and oral muscle movements, cognitive behavioral therapy (CBT) to increase stress tolerance, and occupational therapy, which uses physical activity to help students learn sensory processing skills.

Creating a Sensory-Friendly Classroom

A sensory-friendly classroom is a space that is designed with your students' sensory comfort in mind. This type of classroom environment doesn't only benefit students with ASD but also considers the sensory preferences of students who are suffering from anxiety, PTSD, and ADHD. Moreover, this intentional classroom layout enhances the learning experience of neurotypical students, making it inclusive and accessible to all students regardless of their learning styles.

When creating a sensory-friendly classroom, the best place to start is to make a list of the five senses (i.e., smell, sight, taste, touch, and hearing) and brainstorm modifications that you can make to cater to students' hypersensitivities. In more recent years, doctors have recognized three additional sensory inputs that play a role in how we experience our surroundings. These are balance, movement, and proprioception (or internal body awareness) (Cooke, 2021b). So, in total, there are eight senses that you will need to consider when redesigning your classroom.

Bear in mind that you don't need to spend a lot of money to create a sensory-friendly classroom. Most adjustments like changing the seating arrangement or dimming the lights come at no extra cost. For bigger changes like purchasing comfy beanbags or sensory toys, you will need to consult the head of the department or school administration to determine whether these purchases fall within the classroom budget.

Below are some cost-effective strategies for updating your classroom.

Dim the Lights

Bright fluorescent lighting can be painful for students with sensory issues. Consider dimming the lights to mimic the natural sunlight so students feel alert and energized. If you cannot dim the lights for whatever reason (perhaps you have a student in class with visual impairments), speak to parents and kindly request for them to buy a pair of photophobia glasses for children who may be living with light sensitivity.

Regulate Noise Levels

Students with sensory issues can pick on subtle and loud noises. This becomes a major distraction for them when they are attempting to focus on schoolwork. Identify the recurring sounds that occur inside your classroom and write them down. These may include sounds like giving instructions to students, classroom conversations, pens clicking, pages turning, and so on.

Limit the sounds to only a handful at a time. For instance, when you are giving instructions, students shouldn't be writing anything down. Their hands should be on their laps and their eyes focused on you. When students are working, talking should be kept at a minimum to avoid distractions. Another option for students who get easily triggered by noise is to request that their parents purchase a pair of noise-canceling headphones, which they can wear during work time.

Create a Quiet Zone

Designate a space in your classroom where students can retreat whenever they are experiencing sensory overload. This space should be soothing and consist of comfortable furniture and calming objects. Set strict rules for how students need to behave when they are in the quiet zone to avoid disrupting other students who may be sharing the space with them. For example, you can establish a no-talking or engagement rule in a quiet zone. Students who want to socialize can move to social zones around the classroom.

Minimize the Smells and Scents

Similar to noises, smells can be distracting and overwhelming when there are a lot of them floating in the classroom. Students with sensory issues, particularly those who are hypersensitive, can pick up on faint and pungent smells very easily. To eliminate smells, encourage habits like leaving school bags outside, brushing teeth before school, regularly washing and sanitizing hands, and allowing students to have regular restroom breaks. If you are going to apply perfume or cologne, do so very lightly to avoid carrying the scent across the classroom.

Declutter Your Space

Physical clutter can trigger stress and anxiety for some students. Kindly request that your students help you keep the classroom tidy. Assign cleanup jobs to students, such as picking up the papers on the floor, wiping desks, or returning books and other learning materials where they belong. To avoid injuries, make sure that the pathways are cleared and that there are no school bags or objects causing obstructions. Have students complete a scan of their desks and surroundings before they leave to ensure that they have all of their belongings.

Enhancing the Learning Experience for Students With Sensory Needs

When creating a sensory-friendly classroom, don't forget about improving the sensory-friendly learning experience too. How students receive instructions or engage with the learning material can be stressful for those who are hypersensitive or feel underwhelming for those who are hyposensitive.

The challenge with the traditional learning style is that students are restricted from moving or actively participating in their learning. They are expected to sit still and stay focused on processing what the teacher is saying. Instructions are often given verbally, without alternative methods offered. Students with sensory issues may perceive this type of traditional learning style as rigid or painstakingly boring.

Your teaching methods should be flexible enough to accommodate students' sensory needs so that nobody feels left out. To get them engaged in their learning, they need variety and movement. Below are three strategies to help you recreate this in your classroom.

Sensory-Friendly Learning Experience

Who said that learning needs to be dull and mechanical? To create a sensory-friendly learning experience, give your students options on how they can absorb information. Ask for their input when designing lessons or projects so that you can collect feedback. The aim is to make learning not feel like learning by appealing to a range of students' sensory needs. Here are some tips you can implement:

- **Provide sensory input choices:** Create opportunities for students to choose the most comfortable way to engage with instructions, textbooks, and assignments. Include at least two sensory choices, such as reading text and listening to an audio for each task. Make sure that the content and learning outcomes stay the same so that you don't lower the academic standard.

- **Encourage sensory breaks:** Empower students to listen to their bodies and give themselves breaks whenever they need them. Teach them a hand signal that they can perform to notify you that they need a break. In between tasks, you can allocate 3–5 minutes for students to stretch their legs and take restroom breaks.

- **Integrate technology in lessons:** Use technological tools strategically to add variety to your lessons and cater to students who might have different learning styles. For instance, you might give instructions using interactive whiteboards or have students complete assignments on educational apps. On the other hand, while technology can be exciting, it can also lead to overstimulation. Design tech-free zones in the classroom where students can unplug and ground themselves.

Sensory-Friendly Seating

For students who fidget or have tactile sensitivities, the type and quality of seating in the classroom are important. Traditional classroom chairs might be too hard, flat, or rough for their liking. Flexible seating provides students with alternatives to the traditional classroom chair, such as sitting on beanbags, yoga balls, or cushions.

These alternative options are commonly seen in elementary school classrooms; however, they can be incorporated into middle school and high school classrooms as well. For example, instead of taking away the traditional chairs and desks, you can create a quiet zone that has comfy pillows and chairs for students to lie on.

The purpose of flexible seating is to offer variety so that students aren't sitting in the same position for the entire school day. Some seats can have back support; some could encourage standing; and others could be large fluffy beanbags that encourage laying flat on their stomachs. Switching between these seats can reduce stress and restlessness and promote movement and productivity.

Here are some examples of flexible seating that you can add to your classroom:

- adjustable wobble stools

- stationary stools

- no-roll yoga ball chairs

- chair cushions

- weighted lap pads

- portable lap desks

- standing desks

- kneeling chairs

Consult with an occupational therapist before purchasing flexible seating to assess the best options for your student's sensory needs.

Sensory-Friendly Teaching Instructions

Multisensory learning is an inclusive teaching approach that uses a range of strategies to engage students in the learning process. The aim is to think broadly about how information can be conveyed without relying solely on verbal instructions or written instructions. Remember that students have eight senses that can be stimulated to provide a captivating sensory learning experience.

For example, students can learn through visual aids like pictures, storybooks, reward charts, and diagrams. They can listen to audiobooks or instructions that are repeated slowly and intentionally. Students may learn better by getting their hands involved in activities and by playing with different materials. Some may enjoy getting up from their seats and learning by moving their bodies.

To practice multisensory learning, you must seek to integrate as many sensory learning styles as possible in your activities. This can stimulate different parts of the students' brains and help them retain information. You can use this teaching approach for any topic or subject and at any grade. Some subjects like science, biology, and creative arts support a multisensory learning approach as the normal way to teach.

Group Activity: Sensory Sensitivity Exploration

Place teachers in pairs and assign each group a sensory sensitivity (e.g., visual, light, sound, etc.). Have them spend 15–20 minutes preparing a short presentation on their topic, focusing on how their sensory sensitivity affects students' learning. The aim is to capture the experiences of students and the challenges they might face. After the presentations are over, sit down together and discuss the insights gathered. Brainstorm ideas on how you can address these sensitivities.

Individual Activity: Sensory Sensitivity Reflection Journal

Keep a reflection journal where you document observations of sensory sensitivities in your students throughout the week. Make note of specific sensory triggers, coping behaviors, as well as your own reactions. At the end of the week, reflect on recurring patterns and some of the ways you can address sensory sensitivities in your classroom.

In this chapter, we have discussed the impact of sensory processing issues on students with ASD and explored various strategies to create a sensory-friendly learning and classroom environment. Let's proceed to the next chapter and look at effective ways to handle challenging behaviors in the classroom.

Chapter 5:

Understanding and Responding to Challenging Behaviors

We need to give each other the space to grow, to be ourselves, to exercise our diversity. We need to give each other space so that we may both give and receive such beautiful things as ideas, openness, dignity, joy, healing, and inclusion.

–Max de Pree

Identifying Triggers of Challenging Behaviors

Students in general will occasionally test boundaries and misbehave. This is a normal part of growing up and learning socially acceptable behaviors. Due to the diverse backgrounds of your students, it is also normal for some of them to have trouble following certain rules, as they are not taught them at home or in their cultures.

ASD does not cause bad behavior, however—what can happen instead is that some classroom situations may trigger anxiety, emotional outbursts, or mood swings. Students who are not taught healthy coping mechanisms can resort to aggression, impulsive behaviors, or self-sabotage to express their feelings.

It can be beneficial to find out what upsets students with ASD so that you can find ways to reduce their exposure to triggers. The following scenarios are examples of common classroom scenarios that can be overwhelming for students and potentially lead to challenging behaviors.

Unstructured Time

Students with ASD thrive on structure and routines because that helps them manage transitions and avoid overstimulation. When there are no rules, agendas, or clear limits and boundaries, students can become hyper, impulsive, or restless. Examples of occasions when students may be given unstructured time include

- waiting in line to ride the school bus

- before and after schooltime

- classroom transitions

- recess and eating lunch

- physical education

Academic Challenges

It is common for some students with ASD to experience cognitive delays that cause speech, language, reading, and writing challenges. This can be frustrating, especially when they are noticeably behind their peers. Some of the specific academic challenges that they may encounter include

- understanding instructions
- breaking down tasks
- reading aloud
- writing legibly
- staying organized
- presenting in class
- completing assignments on time
- preparing for tests and exams
- participating in classroom discussions

Sensory Issues

Sensory triggers can happen anywhere and anytime and may impact students' ability to focus and stay motivated in class. These triggers tend to heighten anxiety and cause students to feel a lack of control over their minds and bodies. Common sensory triggers that can occur in the classroom include

- crowded spaces

- loud noises

- sounds of whispers

- sounds of chewing

- unpleasant smells

- uncomfortable clothing

- uncomfortable seating

Social Interactions

Due to the fear of social interactions, some students with ASD may avoid striking conversations with others. When placed in situations where they are forced to speak or engage with you or their classmates, they can feel anxious and panicked, which leads to saying the wrong things or behaving inappropriately. Examples of social interactions that can trigger anxiety include

- being reprimanded publicly

- being asked questions in front of the class

- unplanned speeches or presentations

- changes to daily routines

- school assemblies

- group projects

- initiating conversations with peers

- compromising plans to accommodate others

The Four Functions of Behavior

Now that you know the common triggers for students with ASD, you have a better understanding of where their challenging behaviors stem from. However, this still doesn't explain why some choose to misbehave. Applied Behavioral Analysis (ABA) therapy explains why children act in particular ways by defining four functions of behavior, which are: escape, attention, tangible items, and sensory stimulation (Zauderer, 2023a).

You can trace back challenging behaviors to one or more of these functions and understand the motivation or underlying need behind those behaviors. This is a crucial step to practice before reacting to challenging behaviors or following disciplinary measures. Instead of focusing on the *what*, dig deeper and discover the unspoken *why*. Students do not misbehave for the sake of misbehaving. In most cases, there is something they want that they fail to express in words.

Below is a brief overview of the four functions of behavior and the unspoken needs that they reveal.

Escape

Stress activates the fight–flight–freeze response, which causes students to either confront, escape, or stand frozen when they feel threatened. Escaping is a coping strategy to avoid processing what is happening. Some of the ways that a student escapes is by avoiding eye contact, walking away, putting their head down on the desk, pretending to not hear what is being said, isolating themselves from peers, and so on.

Attention

Some students desire attention whenever they are misbehaving. Therefore, instead of escaping, they might do things that would raise eyebrows, get people talking, and have the spotlight on them. Attention-seeking behaviors are almost always destructive or abnormal because that's how students get noticed. Examples of attention-seeking behaviors include hitting other children, throwing objects, standing on furniture, screaming, taking the opposite action, saying inappropriate words or phrases, and so on. When students don't get the attention they are looking for, they can escalate the behavior until it becomes problematic.

Tangible Items

Another reason why students misbehave is to receive tangible items or privileges. They often make their requests known through attention-seeking behaviors. For example, a student may throw their pencils on the floor because they want to use the tablet to complete their assignment. Another student might throw a tantrum because they want to spend time in the quiet zone rather than working at their desk. Sometimes, offering these tangible items or privileges is not possible, however, you can negotiate a better solution that enables the student to get some of what they are asking for without deviating from the task at hand.

Sensory Stimulation

Challenging behavior can be motivated by pleasure. For instance, a student might daydream because it feels soothing, sing loudly at an inappropriate time because they are bored, or play rough with their peers because they enjoy the painful sensation. The need for sensory stimulation arises when students are bored or disengaged. To entertain themselves, they might turn to behaviors that they consider fun or interesting.

Both good and bad behaviors are a bid to either achieve something or avoid something. Therefore, even the most challenging behaviors are rooted in good intentions. Students will be motivated to learn and adopt good behaviors when they see them as something worth pursuing and achieving.

You can use positive reinforcement to recognize and bring attention to good behaviors, thereby making them more desirable in students' eyes. For example, whenever you catch a student demonstrating patience, you can stop and praise them for their efforts. When this is done regularly (and with sincerity), they begin to desire to show patience in more social contexts.

The Functional Behavior Assessment

If you are concerned about your students' challenging behavior and want to provide more structured support, you can conduct a functional behavior assessment (FBA). The FBA is a process of collecting information about a student's challenging behaviors to understand the causes. Eventually, this evaluation process leads to the creation of the behavior intervention plan (BIP), which is a goal-oriented individualized plan that identifies challenging behaviors and the relevant strategies to address them.

Bear in mind that not all students who display challenging behavior will qualify for an FBA. This assessment is typically offered to students who are being evaluated for special education services or to students who have an IEP and are being assessed for new behavior concerns. Some schools may conduct an FBA as part of their disciplinary procedures, particularly when the behaviors committed are suspected to be linked to a disability of some sort.

Similar to the IEP process, a team is created to conduct an FBA. The team consists of various stakeholders such as the classroom teacher, the school psychologist, certain medical professionals, the student, and family members.

Encouraging Positive Behaviors Using the Positive Behavior Support Framework

Positive Behavior Support (PBS) is an approach that is used to promote behavioral changes in children and adults with disabilities. The focus is not on calling out challenging behaviors or "fixing" the individual, but instead on reinforcing the desired behaviors you want to see. PBS is based on the simple principle that if you can make the desired behavior valuable and accessible, then there won't be an incentive to continue practicing the challenging behavior. PBS also suggests that since challenging behaviors are learned, they can be unlearned and replaced with alternative, positive behaviors.

The PBS plan is a document you can create for students who display challenging behaviors in your classroom. Similar to the FBA, it seeks to understand the cause of the challenging behavior; however, it goes a step further and outlines proactive and reactive strategies that you can use to monitor and address behaviors. Proactive strategies are designed to avoid triggers or disruptions by making sure the student has everything they need to succeed in the classroom environment. Reactive strategies are designed to manage challenging behaviors when they occur and regain control in conflict situations. An effective PBS will include more proactive strategies than reactive strategies because, ultimately, the goal is to equip students with the skills and tools needed to regulate their emotions and feel motivated to learn.

Ideally, the PBS plan will be compiled after an FBA has been carried out. However, when an FBA is not available, you can create individualized PBS plans to get in front of challenging behaviors. When you are ready, follow these steps to create your plan.

Step 1: Identify the Challenging Behavior

Describe the behavior you are seeking to address. It is recommended to focus on one or two behaviors at a time. Mention the characteristics of the behavior to provide more details about what it is, when it happens, how long it lasts, and how it impacts the student and the rest of the classroom.

Step 2: Describe the Functions

Describe the functions of the behavior, that is, the motivations behind it. Refer to the four functions of behavior outlined earlier in the chapter and decide on the best category or categories the behavior falls under. Later on, when you are brainstorming strategies, you will need to ensure that the suggestions you make help to address the different functions. For example, what other ways can you help the student feel seen without resorting to hitting other children?

After the second step, you will begin to think of proactive and reactive strategies. The traffic light analogy is used to describe the levels of interventions that you will go through depending on the student's behavior. **Green** strategies are designed for typical classroom behaviors, **amber** strategies are designed for disruptive behaviors, and red strategies are designed for harmful and unacceptable behaviors. Following every incident, you will be advised to practice blue strategies, which are caring and supportive strategies to help the student return to their normal self.

Step 3: Create Proactive Green Strategies

Green strategies apply to all students who are calm and going about their normal school day. These strategies are considered proactive because they seek to build trusting relationships with students and equip them with the necessary coping skills to monitor and correct their own behaviors. The goal is to help students feel relaxed, motivated, and supported.

When creating green strategies for a specific student, think about how they behave in their normal state of mind. Consider how they look when they are not stressed, anxious, or confused. For example, do they tend to tell jokes, smile, clap their hands, and interact with other children? The strategies that you come up with should assist in keeping the student in this ideal state of mind. Examples of strategies that you can implement include

- using language the student prefers and understands

- providing positive reinforcement

- regularly reminding the student of the rules, routines, and instructions

- being consistent in your actions

- providing regular movement breaks

Step 4: Create Early Warning Amber Strategies

The amber stage is when a student shows the early warning signs of challenging behavior. If you are aware of how they behave in their normal state of mind, you will be able to pick up on sudden changes in their behaviors, such as speaking louder, going silent, being unresponsive, starting unnecessary fights, or complaining. Some signs may be more subtle, such as changes to their body language, pacing around, or facial expressions.

The goal of amber strategies is to reverse the symptoms of stress, anxiety, or hyperarousal and help the student return to their normal state. This is known as de-escalation. Here are examples of amber strategies that you can implement:

- Physically remove the trigger.

- Divert or distract the student.

- Encourage taking deep breaths.

- Do something fun like dancing to ease stress.

- Give the student what they want (if it is okay to do so).

Step 5: Create Reactive Red Strategies

Ideally, we don't want students to reach the red stage because that is when they act out their challenging behaviors. It becomes increasingly difficult to manage students' behaviors when they are impulsive, chaotic, and making other children feel threatened. Remember that behind challenging behaviors are functions. Students who "act out" are motivated by something they want or something they are trying to avoid.

The goal of red strategies is to bring an immediate end to the challenging behavior while making sure that everyone is safe in the process. Here, you need to react quickly to avoid allowing the crisis to become worse. Strategies that you can practice include

- talking in a calm and monotone voice

- being mindful of your body language

- avoiding threatening language or making demands

- using space to provide enough distance between you and the student

- enforcing consequences without entertaining any back-and-forth conversations

Reactive strategies need to be ordered in such a way that they gradually increase in intensity. For example, try low-arousal and noninvasive strategies before you proceed to restrictive and invasive strategies.

Step 6: Create Post-Incident Blue Strategies

The blue stage is the recovery and support stage that occurs after the incident. To maintain strong and healthy relationships with your students, it is important to show that you still care about them, even after they have behaved poorly. Providing support can also help students regulate their nervous systems and return to a calm and balanced state.

The goal of blue strategies is to help the student calm down. However, you must be careful not to trigger them with your words or actions, leading to a sudden behavior escalation again. Be mindful of the time and space the student needs to regain control of their mind and body. Every student will have their own way of self-soothing, so learn what they do to cope and show respect for their process. Examples of blue strategies that you can implement include

- giving the student time to process their feelings

- physically moving to a different area of the classroom

- sifting the mood in the classroom by introducing a fun activity

- offering warm smiles and positive body language to show support

- calling the student aside and reflecting on the incident together

Step 7: Review and Get an Agreement on the Plan From All Stakeholders

Once you have compiled the PBS plan, run it past the student's parents and other relevant stakeholders to get their approval. It is also necessary to explain the PBS plan to the student involved using age-appropriate language. Focus on explaining the purpose of the plan and the proactive and reactive strategies you will use to help them cope with strong emotions and challenging behaviors. Schedule periodic reviews of the PBS plan to assess whether the strategies are helping to address the challenging behaviors. Make modifications to the plan whenever they are needed.

Group Activity: Functions of Behavior Analysis

Go around the circle and ask each teacher to present an example of a student who displayed challenging behavior in their classroom. Ask them to detail what the behavior was, how frequently it happened, and what function it served.

Individual Activity: Positive Behavior Support Practice

Create a PBS plan for a specific student exhibiting challenging behaviors in your classroom. You are also welcome to create a plan for a fictional student. Come up with tailored strategies based on the student's unique needs, triggers, and functions of behavior.

In this chapter, we have taken a deep dive into challenging behaviors in the classroom and examined different ways to address them. We can now proceed to the next chapter and discuss useful strategies to teach students self-regulation skills.

Chapter 6:

Strategies for Promoting Self-Regulation

If they can't learn the way we teach, we teach the way they learn.
—O. Ivar Lovaas

Teaching Self-Calming Techniques

Time spent at school is not always a bed of roses. Some days are fun and productive, while other days are long and strenuous. It's normal for students to be moody, irritable, or disinterested in classroom topics and lessons. However, what's not acceptable is for them to act out whenever they are not feeling their best. Your role as a teacher is to create a calm and motivating environment that can enhance learning, but students are responsible for managing their own behaviors.

Self-calming techniques are soothing ways for students to manage their strong emotions and challenging behaviors. Essentially, these techniques reverse the symptoms of stress and allow students to slowly return to their balanced self. From an infantile age, children teach themselves how to regulate their nervous systems by doing things like sucking their thumbs, rocking their bodies, or humming. These self-calming techniques help them cope with discomfort in new situations or in the absence of their parents.

Some children forget these techniques when they grow up and go into panic mode whenever they encounter stressful situations. Others adopt unhelpful forms of self-calming like self-isolation or emotional avoidance. At the moment, they may feel an instant relief from stress, but later on, they may face the same triggering issues and may struggle to cope with their emotions.

Self-calming techniques come with many benefits for students with ASD. The major benefit is that these techniques activate the parasympathetic nervous system, which is the mechanism that turns off the fight–flight–freeze mode and allows them to enter a state of rest. Due to their ongoing battles with anxiety, students with ASD can feel less stressed, impulsive, or panicked when they practice self-calming techniques. Another benefit is that students build their stress tolerance and learn to withstand pain and discomfort without making regrettable decisions. The techniques encourage present-moment awareness and focus on what can be done now to alleviate distress.

We can classify self-calming techniques as proactive strategies to prevent or reduce emotional discomfort. They work best when they are practiced before challenging behavior manifests or during the recovery stage, rather than in the middle of a crisis. Students cannot soothe themselves while they are triggered. They need to calm down for a while and regain a sense of control to engage in these types of techniques.

ASD-Friendly Self-Calming Techniques to Practice in the Classroom

Learning about your students' personalities and behaviors can make it easier for you to identify students who are struggling. Not every student will be loud and disruptive when they are experiencing anxiety or sensory overload. Some will become quiet and look "checked out." Respond to students immediately when you notice early signs of distress and suggest self-calming techniques that can help them calm down. Below are some of the techniques you can present.

Provide Sensory Toys and Objects

Sensory toys and objects can be a great way to distract students during the early stages of a meltdown. The objective is to redirect their focus from their unwanted thoughts or emotions to the slimy, cold, coarse, or musical object in front of them. Find a large storage box and place it in the quiet zone of the classroom (where students retreat to ground themselves). Fill the box with a bunch of sensory toys and objects, which could include sunglasses, candy wrappers, building blocks, stuffed animals, Play-Doh, musical instruments, bottles of bubbles, and so on.

Offer an Escape

Sometimes the best thing you can do for students who feel overwhelmed is to give them permission to take a walk and get some fresh air. This can be helpful when the classroom is loud and they cannot self-regulate with all of the sensory commotion happening. Taking a walk can also provide a mental break from focusing on difficult tasks. For example, if you can see that a student is struggling to complete their work, send them on an errand to the office so they get an opportunity to recenter themselves.

Distract With Special Interests

Another way to distract students who appear distressed is to ask them questions about their special interests. Once again, the aim is to redirect their focus away from the troubling thoughts and emotions to the things they are passionate about. Show genuine curiosity about their favorite topics, share information that you have recently found, or present a task that involves their special interests.

Practice Breathing Techniques

Deep breathing is a technique that allows more oxygen into the body to induce a state of relaxation. What's great about deep breathing is that every student knows how to perform the exercise. They simply need to take slow and long breaths, inhaling through the nose and exhaling out the mouth. Each breath should reach the belly before being released. Breathing techniques can be done as a group exercise with all students in the classroom, before and after class time. Stand in front of the class and lead them through a simple technique such as box breathing, repeating the exercise several times before moving on to the next activity.

Take the Lesson Outside

Exposure to natural sunlight and movement can significantly lower stress and boost positive emotions. Whenever you notice that your students look bored or disengaged, take the lesson outside and find a cool area where students can work, conduct experiments, or complete group projects. Before lessons, you can take students outside for a quick physical workout. Physical activity releases endorphins and can make students feel more confident. Turn the workout into a challenge to make it fun. For instance, to gain access to the classroom, students need to do five jumping jacks.

Adopt a Classroom Pet

Having a classroom pet creates a sense of community and gives students a common object to focus on. Small furry animals can also provide sensory stimulation to anxious students and improve their overall well-being. Whenever they are feeling overwhelmed, they can walk over to the pet and play with it. Furthermore, students will look forward to taking turns looking after the pet over weekends.

Note that not all of these strategies will work in every context. Take some time to assess the situation, as well as the student's behavior, before deciding on which self-calming technique to suggest.

Fostering Emotional Awareness

Students need to be encouraged to speak up whenever they are upset or uncomfortable. Whenever they do this, they can gain perspective on their troubling situations and find proactive ways to manage their emotions. One of the reasons why students fail to express their emotions is that they don't have the vocabulary to describe what they are experiencing. Help students identify and name their emotions, to foster emotional awareness.

Emotional awareness refers to skills related to the identification, classification, and communication of emotions. These skills are taught and emphasized in elementary school; however, they are useful throughout students' schooling careers and in other aspects of their lives. It's important for teachers to not assume that older students know how to articulate their feelings, because some students' brains mature later than others. Additionally, emotional awareness isn't a skill that is always reinforced by parents in some homes. This means that the only exposure some students have to the skill is when they are coached at school. Therefore, it is necessary to go over emotional awareness skills regularly to ensure they can confidently practice them.

Below are some strategies that you can present to students to help them improve their emotional awareness skills.

Big vs. Small Problems

Help students understand differences in the size and weight of problems. Teach them that problems come in all shapes and require different amounts of attention. For example, a child refusing to share their toys has a different weight than a child expressing hurtful words. The latter is more serious and requires more attention. Play a game where students need to rate problems on a scale from 1–5 and discuss the appropriate responses for these problems. Highlight instances where responses would be overreactions or underreactions.

Expand Emotional Range

To increase students' emotional vocabulary, create activities where they are required to use a range of emotions to convey messages. For instance, you can present a worksheet that asks students to look at different facial expressions and write down the emotion represented. For older students, you can ask them to journal about their best and worst childhood memories or analyze the biography of a famous person and the journey they went through to become successful.

Picture Books

Younger students can learn more about identifying and labeling emotions by reading picture books or being asked questions about the experiences of various characters. This could also be a great lesson in showing empathy. For instance, you can ask students to put themselves in the character's shoes and imagine how they would handle their situations. Another strategy is to ask students to observe the character's body language and reflect on what they might be feeling at the moment.

Gratitude Circles

Spend the first few minutes or the last few minutes of the class in bringing students together and forming a circle. Go around the circle and ask students to mention something they are grateful for without repeating what has already been mentioned. Practicing gratitude is a powerful way to reflect on emotions and feel grounded in the present moment. It can also relieve stress and overthinking, allowing students to focus on what's going well in their lives.

Appreciation, Apology, Aha!

Another perspective-taking and gratitude exercise that works best at the end of the school day is asking students to mention something they have appreciated, discovered, and needed to apologize for. This provides a daily opportunity for students to reflect on their interactions and behaviors. On some days, students won't need to make apologies; however, when they do, encourage them to do so before parting ways with their peers.

Private Check-Ins With Students

Some students may feel uncomfortable sharing their emotions in public interactions. When you notice this, do not force them to open up. Instead, schedule a private check-in with them to go through the emotional awareness exercises together and find out how they are doing. Pay attention to their responses and make notes of things you would like to follow up with them on. Give them uninterrupted time to verbalize their thoughts and feelings, and validate them. If you detect problems, write them down and keep track of their behaviors. Schedule follow-up check-ins when necessary.

Emotional awareness skills get better with time once students develop greater self-awareness and comfort in their emotions. Continue to create opportunities for your students to engage with their emotions in low-stress environments to master these skills.

Group Activity: Create Self-Regulation Charts

Work with other teachers to create self-regulation charts that teach students how to manage strong emotions, practice breathing techniques, and calm themselves when they are feeling overwhelmed. Incorporate visual elements such as pictures or symbols to make the charts visually appealing. Share the charts among yourselves and regularly swap charts to expose your students to different strategies.

Individual Activity: Take a Mindful Walk

Take your students on a mindful walk around the school or outside in nature. Give them instructions to pay attention to their surroundings using their senses (e.g., sight, hearing, smell, touch). As they walk, remind students to focus on their breathing, bringing their attention back to the present moment whenever their minds wander.

In this chapter, we have looked into various self-regulation strategies that are effective for managing stress and anxiety in the classroom. Let's proceed to the next chapter and discuss two areas of particular concern to students with ASD, which are managing anxiety and developing executive function skills.

Chapter 7:

Addressing Anxiety and Executive Function Challenges

The most interesting people you'll find are ones that don't fit into your average cardboard box. They'll make what they need, they'll make their own boxes.
–Dr. Temple Grandin

Recognizing Anxiety Symptoms in Students With ASD

Throughout the book, we have referred to the prevalence of anxiety among students with ASD. Research estimates that as much as 40%–50% of people diagnosed with autism will also receive a diagnosis of anxiety (National Autistic Society, n.d.). The reason for these high levels of anxiety is due to ASD symptoms such as sensory issues or difficulties in socializing with others.

Healthy expressions of anxiety, such as feeling scared before a presentation or nervous to initiate conversations with peers, aren't something that needs to be attended to. Students can manage their emotions by practicing self-regulation strategies to return to their normal selves. However, anxiety becomes a serious concern when it starts to interfere with students' ability to learn, complete classwork, or form positive peer relationships. This is usually when you need to step in and provide support.

Intervene when the following symptoms start to directly impact students' ability to complete tasks or engage in classroom discussions:

- abnormal amounts or lack of eye contact

- ritualistic and repetitive behaviors

- resistance to change

- refusal to follow instructions

The main reason why you should intervene at this point is to prevent an escalation of challenging behaviors. Remember that students who display anxiety are responding to something they want or something they seek to avoid. The type of anxiety they exhibit could shed more light on the function of their behavior. For instance, students who have certain phobias want to escape unusual or triggering stimuli, whereas students with separation anxiety want to feel safe and nurtured. Therefore, you can take proactive steps to respond to the students' needs to prevent ongoing frustration.

Teaching Coping Skills for Anxiety

In the previous chapter, we went through different self-regulation strategies that can help students cope with stress and anxiety. In this section, we are going to explore a few more strategies that deal specifically with anxiety management. These strategies may or may not work in various social contexts and with various students, so assess the situation before deciding which strategies to implement.

Create and Enforce Classroom Values

When students step into your classroom, they should feel at ease and accepted for who they are. Work together with students to create values for your classroom. These are core principles that are represented in classroom interactions. Come up with a maximum of five values so that students can easily memorize them. They can include things like patience, kindness, respect, and acceptance. Explain to students what these values mean and how they can practice them in the classroom. Create a rewards system to recognize and praise students who demonstrate these values.

Make Adjustments to Classroom Policies

Students who are diagnosed with anxiety or display severe anxiety issues cannot simply "get over" their fears and worries. Their anxiety is chronic and gets in the way of focusing and participating in the classroom. Therefore, it is necessary to adjust classroom policies to accommodate these students. The purpose of these adjustments should be to relieve stress while continuing to hold students accountable.

Here are examples of nondisruptive adjustments that you can make:

- Allow students to present to the teacher alone rather than in front of the class.

- Allow students to switch seats when they struggle to concentrate around certain classmates.

- Allow students to sit at an independent desk when they have sensory issues related to physical proximity to other students.

- Give students an additional five minutes to complete assignments for normal classroom assessments (during formal exams, however, they will need to adhere to the strict time restrictions).

- Notify students in advance when they are going to be required to present, answer questions, or work on group projects.

Promote Positive Self-Talk

Teach students how to speak positively about their abilities. For instance, you can encourage them to replace negative words like "can't" or "won't" with positive words like "can" and "will." This could be behavior that you model during classroom discussions too. For example, when giving instructions, you can express how much faith you have in your students to complete the given task. You might say, "I know that it looks difficult, but I know that you can do it!" Another way to model positive self-talk is to ask students to reflect on something they did well during class. They can complete the following statement: "I am proud of myself for [insert positive experience]."

Please note that if students continue to battle with anxiety, they must get additional support outside of the classroom. Enquire about the possibility of enrolling them into a special education program and speak to their parents about working collaboratively with the school counselor and other child specialists who can provide personalized care.

Supporting Executive Function Skills

You may have heard of the term executive function when referring to specific cognitive skills that students may be lacking. The frontal region of the brain, known as the prefrontal cortex, is responsible for executive function skills, which are a set of skills that have to do with an individual's ability to plan, coordinate, and manage high-level tasks.

Naturally, as students reach higher grades, they are taught executive function skills. However, not all of them grab a hold of these skills. Research indicates that up to 80% of people living with ASD will suffer from executive function disorder (Bennie, 2018). This means that some students in your classroom may have challenges completing tasks that require planning, organization, time management, problem-solving, memorization, and reasoning (to name a few).

The only way for students to improve executive function skills is to continually practice them in different contexts. Below is a breakdown of the most common executive function skills and suggestions on how you can reinforce them in the classroom.

Working Memory Skills

Students who are on the spectrum may find it hard to recall information. The irony of this, however, is they have no trouble memorizing information related to their special interests. In essence, the less interesting or stimulating the information, the harder it becomes to remember. You can also see this play out in the routines students can easily follow without guidance versus the ones they need a lot of support to perform, or the school subjects students they perform well in versus the subjects where they perform poorly.

Tips to enhance students' working memory skills include

- playing memory games such as telephone

- breaking down instructions into steps

- using visual aids to emphasize a message

- using easy-to-follow language

- reviewing and reteaching information-dense lessons

- getting students to actively participate in learning

Organizational Skills

It is common for some students with ASD to have trouble staying organized. This can be a problem since clutter or missing items can lead to stress and overstimulation. To feel calm and have a greater sense of control over their environment, students need to develop effective organizational skills.

Tips that you can practice in the classroom include

- helping students label and assign a box or folder for their books and belongings

- using visual aids like posters or infographics to illustrate the steps to perform more involved organizational tasks like studying for tests

- assigning a color to each student and asking parents to wrap their school items using the specific color. The color will correspond to their assigned folders and storage boxes

- introducing students to schedules and making sure that they are aware of the sequence of tasks and events for each day

- staying organized and modeling effective time management skills to help students feel at ease

Attention Skills

The ability to pay attention is associated with memory and concentration skills. Students with ASD may have no trouble focusing on a particular task; however, switching their focus to something else can be challenging. The same goes for students who have a preference for certain sensory inputs like lights, smells, or sounds. They may become fixated on these inputs and have a tough time redirecting their attention to other inputs in their environment.

The following tips can enhance students' attention skills:

- Design lessons based on students' favorite topics and interests.

- Consider incorporating flexible seating options to minimize physical distractions.

- Keep the layout of the classroom simple to avoid visual clutter.

- Provide simple instructions that are easy to follow and memorize.

- Use "First... then..." when giving directions to support task completion.

- Play games that require attention like Simon Says.

Planning Skills

Planning refers to the ability to foresee future needs and take the necessary steps or actions to prepare for them. Successful planning requires a range of executive function skills like attention, working memory, time management, and organization. It can also encourage students to prioritize tasks, making decisions on what to do now versus what to do later.

Here are tips on how you can teach planning skills in the classroom:

- Help students create, structure, and execute academic goals.

- Show students how to create study or homework timetables and prioritize information to learn.

- Provide students with choices and explain the consequences of certain actions.

- Create self-monitoring checklists that students can use and refer to after completing tasks or when assessing their classroom behaviors.

- Use visible timers in the classroom to help students manage time wisely.

Problem-Solving Skills

Some students with ASD may struggle to cope with the challenges brought on by their condition. Those who lack problem-solving skills may turn to unhelpful coping strategies to manage their emotions and actions. By teaching students problem-solving skills, you can help them navigate through social and academic challenges in the most proactive and productive way. Furthermore, they will be empowered to take ownership of their learning or social interactions and feel motivated to change.

The following will enhance students' problem-solving skills:

- Use role-play to reenact act out everyday scenarios and help students address the challenges.

- Create an opportunity for students to gather themselves and collect their thoughts whenever they appear to be overwhelmed.

- Create an area in the classroom where students can retreat to self-regulate.

- Create social stories to help students manage their anxiety around some school-related situations.

- Ask students open-ended questions to gather insights and feedback.

- Use positive reinforcement and rewards to recognize effective decision-making.

What students need to know is that they are smart and capable of making the right choices inside and outside of the classroom. Create opportunities for students to showcase their cognitive strengths and praise them every time they do. Developing executive function skills will take longer for students with ASD, so have patience and teach them to be gentle with themselves as well.

Group Activity: Create a Coping Toolbox

Set up and host an interactive, hands-on workshop where teachers learn about executive function skills and get to create their own classroom coping toolbox. The toolbox should be an anxiety management kit filled with items and resources to support students who are feeling anxious. Some of the materials that you can provide on the day include stress balls, notebooks for journaling, fidget toys, affirmation cards, calming music, and written mindfulness exercises with pictures. Encourage teachers to provide feedback on how their students received the toolbox.

Individual Activity: Executive Function Skills Inventory

Reflect on your own executive function skills by assessing your executive function strengths and weaknesses. Think about how these strengths and weaknesses may impact your ability to support students with ASD. Set meaningful goals and identify specific skills you can prioritize for development, such as organization, time management, and problem-solving. Reach out to a teacher who can be your accountability partner and offer support along the way.

In this chapter, we have discussed the role and impact of anxiety and executive function problems on students with ASD and outlined effective strategies to address these challenges in the classroom. Let us now move on to the next chapter and discuss ways to help students enhance their social skills.

Chapter 8:

Social Skills Development for Students with ASD

Children with autism are colorful they are often very beautiful and, like the rainbow, they stand out.
–Adele Devine

Understanding Social Interaction Difficulties in ASD

You have learned that students with ASD have challenges with social interactions and communication, but what does this mean? ASD is both a neurological and developmental condition, which means that it causes brain changes and developmental delays or impairments. As a result, some students on the spectrum may exhibit emotional and behavioral issues that affect their ability to socialize effectively with others.

When we speak of social interaction difficulties, we are referring to several challenges that students may encounter which affect their ability to build and maintain healthy and reciprocal relationships. Two types of social interaction difficulties that are often associated with ASD are lack of communication and relationship-building skills.

Communication

Some students with ASD may have trouble with receptive and expressive language skills, meaning that they struggle to understand and interpret verbal messages as well as express their thoughts and emotions in appropriate ways. Not only can these challenges affect their ability to listen to and follow instructions, but they can also create anxiety around initiating or maintaining conversations with peers. On a more advanced level, older students may misinterpret or fail to pick up on social cues, body language, facial expressions, tone of voice, or figures of speech (e.g., sarcasm), which causes communication barriers with others.

Relationship-Building

Students with ASD find it difficult to know what appropriate or inappropriate behavior looks like based on the feedback they are given. Unless they are told and reminded to share their toys, take turns speaking, or ask questions to show interest in others, they cannot intuitively know how to do this. They are often seen as uncooperative due to their lack of negotiation, reciprocity, and collaboration skills. Students with ASD are often caught off guard by the negative feedback they get from teachers and classmates because of their inability to read social cues and modify their behaviors accordingly.

The consequences of not developing positive social skills are plenty. Students with ASD may either choose to isolate themselves from their peers or they may be excluded by their peers. When students are not taught to embrace differences, their response is to reject what they find abnormal. Facing social rejection can negatively impact students' self-worth and sense of belonging. Some may develop social anxiety or depression as a result of their exclusion. Eventually, students who are seen as being different and excluded from the group may become the target of bullying of all forms. This can aggravate or worsen social anxiety and make it increasingly difficult to concentrate and thrive at school.

How to Teach Students Social Communication Skills

It can be tough for students to engage and participate in the classroom without the necessary social and communication skills. Remember that these skills are not only useful for building relationships but are also necessary for seeking clarity, asking questions, following directions, and feeling confident to perform tasks.

Two effective therapies that can help students develop social communication skills are social skills training and applied behavior analysis (ABA). Social skills training involves teaching social skills through modeling, role-playing, and providing explicit instructions. Specific ASD-related challenges are addressed, such as the ability to take turns, take on different perspectives, and improve conversational skills. ABA, on the other hand, is a systematic behavioral approach that can identify and modify unwanted behaviors through positive reinforcement and positive behavior support (PBS). Social expectations are broken down into smaller steps and clear instructions are given to help students practice the appropriate behaviors.

Two additional school-based interventions can assist students in developing social communication skills. The first is creating and sharing social stories in the classroom to describe different social interactions and the appropriate ways to behave in those contexts. This works well with younger students who need to be taught social rules and expectations like greetings, having good manners, and showing interest in others. The second is peer-mediated interventions where you create opportunities for students to interact with their peers and build positive relationships. Group tasks and activities like taking turns and working collaboratively to solve problems can be designed to address specific social challenges.

When it comes to teaching social skills in the classroom, target one skill at a time and follow these simple steps:

1. Introduce the skill to students by explaining what it is. Use social stories, rules, and videos to get them familiar with the skill and interested in learning more about it.

2. Go deeper and describe the characteristics of the skill, as well as how and when to practice it. Use games, visual aids, or demonstrations to show students what the skill looks like in action.

3. Allow students to practice the skill. Divide them into smaller groups to allow them to discuss and exchange ideas about the skill, then present it to the class or submit an assignment related to the skill.

4. Show students how they can apply the skill in different social settings. Use role-play to demonstrate various scenarios where the skill might be beneficial. Once

again, students can actively participate to engage in the learning.

There are a variety of social skills that you can introduce and teach to students at different developmental ages. Below is a list that you can refer to.

Listening and Taking Turns to Speak

Listening is a big component of effective communication. Good listening skills enable students to hear and fully comprehend the message that is being relayed and respond appropriately. Teach students how to be good listeners by encouraging them to

- practice making and sustaining eye contact.

- listen carefully to the words that are being spoken.

- think about what they have just heard.

- wait patiently until the other person has finished talking before they reply.

Use visual charts to illustrate the step-by-step process of listening during conversations. To practice listening skills, ask students to role-play being good listeners. Have them switch between the roles of speaker and listener to understand both perspectives. You can even bring a wooden spoon and tell students to only speak once they are given the wooden spoon.

Requesting Help

Students will need help from you or your peers occasionally, and it is perfectly normal and encouraged for them to ask for it. Nevertheless, there is a method to ask for help to ensure positive feedback and results. Below are the steps that you can present and practice with your students:

1. Identify the problem you are having.

2. Think about possible solutions on your own.

3. If you cannot solve the problem on your own, think of the right person to help you.

4. Check with the person to see if they have a moment to speak with you.

5. State the problem you are having and make a specific request.

6. Listen carefully to the advice or instructions.

7. Take notes to summarize what you have just heard.

8. Repeat the advice or instruction back to the person to clarify the message.

9. Thank the person for helping you.

Social stories are great tools to use when showing students different social scenarios where they might need help and demonstrating the correct and incorrect ways of asking for help. You can also create a poster to show students whom to contact when they are facing specific issues.

Initiating Play

Another crucial social skill that students will need to learn is how to initiate and maintain play. Note that "play" will look different for a student in elementary school compared to a student in high school; however, the same rules apply. Students need to learn how to approach their peers and engage in conversations or suggest activities. Below is an exercise that you can present to your students to teach them how to practice the skill:

- Divide students into pairs and have them face each other, standing at a distance of about five feet.

- Assign students the letters A and B. In the first round, all of the As will be initiators and the Bs will be responders.

- Provide specific steps that the initiators must follow to initiate play. For example, the first step might be making eye contact with the responder, then approaching them, then greeting them with a smile, and then asking a question to initiate play.

- Provide instructions for how the responders must reply. These can also be given in steps. Ensure the reply is always positive, even when declining the invitation.

Ask the students to switch roles and practice being on the other side. Have them repeat the same process to see how it feels. When students have practiced both roles, sit down with the group and discuss their experiences.

Reading Social Cues

Learning how to read social cues can minimize misunderstandings and awkward social situations and instead promote fulfilling relationships. Students should learn that not every message is spoken using words; some messages are passed through nonverbal communication. When teaching students about social cues, introduce them to the four categories: facial expressions, vocal pitch and tone, body language, and personal space. Since these categories are quite big, split them into different lessons and activities. For example, you can spend a week exploring facial expressions and another week exploring vocal pitch and tone.

Modeling videos, visual charts, and role-play are great tools that you can use to help students recognize social cues. For example, you can create a poster with different emojis representing different facial expressions and what they mean. For older students, you can find videos that help them identify positive and negative body language and the messages being conveyed. Social games are also a fun way of practicing reading social cues. Examples of games that are appropriate in the classroom include Emotional Charade and Monkey See, Monkey Do.

Facilitating Peer Interactions and Friendship Skills

The ability to build and maintain friendships allows students to develop a healthy and stable sense of self that allows them to flourish beyond the school environment. Living with ASD should not get in the way of students forming trusting friendships with their peers. One of your duties as a teacher is to create opportunities for students to interact with each other and participate in classroom activities. Of course, this should be done with students' personalities and comfort levels in mind. Consider implementing the following strategies to promote positive peer interactions in your classroom.

Assign Classroom Jobs

Help students feel like they are valued members of the class by giving them small responsibilities to complete around the classroom. The aim is not to make them work hard but to feel a sense of ownership of their space. Moreover, completing these small responsibilities allows them to feel a sense of accomplishment. Examples of the jobs you can assign include handing out papers, being a line leader, taking attendance, and leading classroom meetings. Create a roster to make sure that every student gets a turn to handle a classroom responsibility.

Create Small and Large Group Activities

Whenever possible, create activities that students can carry out in pairs or larger groups. Group work reinforces several social skills such as collaboration, negotiation, positive conflict resolution, listening, and perspective-taking. To create more structure in group activities, outline different roles that are necessary to complete the assignments, and let students decide among themselves which roles they will take on. Smaller groups can be used for assignments that require critical thinking, whereas larger groups are great for carrying out creative projects and group discussions.

Big Buddies System

Another way to help students feel comfortable interacting with each other is to expose them to older students—big buddies— who can help them develop effective conversational skills and feel confident expressing themselves. Big buddies can be students who are two to three grades higher than your students. The developmental age gap is necessary to help students gain new social skills. Since this type of system needs careful planning, it could be something that you do once or twice every term. Students can also write letters to their big buddies when physical meetups are not possible. Ensure that the letters coming in and going out are moderated before being passed onto students.

Host Classroom Meetings

Classroom meetings are a great way to bring students together and teach them how to read social cues, solve problems collectively, and practice diplomacy. You can decide how often you would like to host classroom meetings and how to structure them. These meetings can be used for sharing announcements, reminders, upcoming changes to routines, birthday shoutouts (and other forms of recognition), and addressing classroom concerns. Students can take turns hosting the meetings, however, provide a standard format and set of instructions or prompts that they can follow to lower their anxiety and make the meetings more predictable.

Group Activity: Host a Social Skills Workshop

Organize and host a social skills workshop where teachers collaborate to develop a series of social skills lessons or activities tailored to the needs of students. Encourage teachers to brainstorm and share their ideas so that you can come up with practical strategies that address specific social skill deficits in the classroom.

Individual Activity: One-on-One Roleplay With Students

Identify students in your classroom with social and communication challenges. Schedule one-on-one role-playing sessions with them and provide prompts and guidance as they practice social skills such as making eye contact, initiating conversation, or asking for help. Offer targeted feedback and positive reinforcement to help them build confidence and feel competent in various social settings.

In this chapter, we have looked at the significance of social and communication skills in improving students' academic and social lives. The strategies outlined in the chapter can increase students' engagement in classroom interactions and facilitate healthy peer relationships.

We have now completed the second part of the book, which focuses on managing ASD-related behaviors in the classroom. We can now proceed to the third part of the book and focus on specific ASD-friendly communication strategies to adopt when instructing students who are on the spectrum.

PART 3:

ASD-Friendly Instructions in the Classroom

Chapter 9:

Communicating Effectively With Students on the Spectrum

I might hit developmental and societal milestones in a different order than my peers, but I am able to accomplish these small victories on my own time.
–Haley Moss

Enhancing Receptive Language Skills

There are two types of language skills that students need to develop: expressive and receptive language. Expressive language refers to the ability to articulate thoughts and feelings, and receptive language refers to the ability to understand and interpret verbal and nonverbal communication. Some students with ASD may show deficits in one or both of these language skills. In this chapter, we will focus on strategies that can help students develop and enhance receptive language skills.

Receptive language often develops before expressive language because, before one can speak, one must gain an understanding of social context and nonverbal cues. Oftentimes, teachers find that students ask questions that were answered in the given instructions. However, due to their inability to understand the rules or expectations, they feel ill-equipped to complete the tasks at hand.

Receptive language skills teach students how to process information accurately so that there are no communication barriers when relaying messages. Some of the things that students learn how to do include:

- following directions

- interpreting visual or audio cues

- identifying objects and symbols

- understanding abstract concepts

- responding to questions

- understanding the lessons of a story

It can be challenging for teachers to gauge whether students truly understand the information being presented to them. Many students nod and confirm that they understand, however, they are simply responding to the prompt (e.g., saying yes when asked, "Do you understand?") and don't entirely know what to do with the information. Some students will visibly show their lack of understanding by avoiding eye contact, appearing dazed, or losing focus. Other students may be good at masking their lack of understanding but will give it away through their poor academic performance.

Fortunately, there are interventions you can implement to make sure that students have access to information and feel empowered to use it appropriately. Here are some of the ways to enhance receptive language skills.

Encourage Eye Contact

Students focus better when they are looking at you while you speak or viewing the visual aid or video that is being presented to them. Before giving instructions, make sure that everyone is looking at you. Deliver instructions in an interesting or entertaining way to encourage engagement. Frequently stop to ensure everyone is still focused on you during your presentation.

Minimize Distractions

It is normal for students to break focus every once in a while. The main reason for this is that they are getting distracted by stimuli in their surroundings. For example, a student might break focus when their classmates start whispering about something or when they feel a cold breeze entering the classroom. Do your best to minimize distractions. Focus on the most disturbing distractions like bright lights, extreme temperatures, clutter on desks, and conversations in the classroom.

Practice Imitation

Get students to repeat information after you. This can enhance their learning and keep them engaged for longer. Use imitation when teaching concepts that involve lengthy processes or language that might be confusing to students. Pronounce the words or sentences slowly and prompt students to copy you. After several rounds of imitation, have students repeat the words or sentences on their own.

Break Down Instructions

Students with ASD may experience trouble memorizing information. For instance, they may be able to understand instructions when they are being communicated, but immediately forget what to do when it's time to take action. Breaking down instructions into steps can help students recall the information better. Their brains can memorize the sequence and use that to remember what steps to take. Use simple numbered steps to show the order of tasks and events. Refrain from adding too many steps, however, as this can create confusion and become counterproductive.

Receptive Language Activities

Students can learn receptive language skills while having fun. For instance, reading picture books to students helps them practice active listening and identify objects and pictures. When reading, pause and ask questions to allow for moments of reflection and create dialogue. Another strategy is to repeat schedules to students to get them familiar with their routines and the sequence of tasks within. For example, before you start teaching, you can go through the agenda for the day and the transitions that students will go through. To assess understanding, you can also give students a quiz to complete after introducing them to new concepts or have students volunteer to play the role of the teacher and present the concepts to the rest of the class.

Utilizing Augmentative and Alternative Communication Systems

Augmentative and alternative communication (AAC) refers to conveying messages in a manner that doesn't involve speech. Alternative communicative methods such as nonverbal gestures, visual aids, and technology provide additional support to learning. The benefit of incorporating AAC in your teaching practice is that you can appeal to students' different learning needs. Students who don't respond well to verbal communication can be given instructions using alternative methods.

There are two categories of AAC that you can apply in your teaching. The first is non-aided AAC, which consists of a range of alternative communication methods that don't require special tools or equipment. In most cases, your physical body is the only tool that you use to convey messages. Some examples of non-aided AAC include facial expressions, gestures, pointing at objects, and body language. The second category is aided AAC, which consists of electronic and paper-based alternative communication methods. For example, electronic books, educational apps, visual posters, and picture books are examples of aided AAC.

AAC can help students with ASD understand information better. However, they can also assist with expressive language skills such as improving speech and articulation of words or forming ideas and communicating them without depending on spoken language. Since no student with ASD is the same, it is important to experiment with different AAC systems to understand which approaches work best for most students.

Three AAC systems are commonly used within the autism community. These are the picture exchange communication system (PECS), language acquisition through motor planning (LAMP), and aided AAC.

Picture Exchange Communication System (PECS)

PECS is an alternative communication system that uses the exchange of pictures to communicate with nonverbal students or students who exhibit speech and language problems. Pictures are presented as prompts to get students to respond with an appropriate picture. Originally, PECS was designed to be used by students in kindergarten who hadn't developed useful language skills. Over time, this method has been used with students of diverse ages and abilities. For example, a student in high school can use PECS to learn how to initiate conversations with their peers or express their wants and needs.

Language Acquisition Through Motor Planning (LAMP)

LAMP is an alternative communication system specifically designed for autistic people and those with other developmental disabilities. It can help students with limited speech or receptive language challenges to practice using or recognizing words by pressing different buttons on a speech-generating device. What makes this system effective is that students learn that the "rule" of producing certain words is consistent regardless of how many times they push the button. Moreover, the rule that applies to one word will not apply to another word. Therefore, students enhance their ability to recognize and understand a wide range of sounds and vocabulary.

Aided AAC

Aided alternative communication relies on objects, pictures, charts, symbols, and electronic devices (or software) to convey messages. Choosing the appropriate aided AAC systems requires you to first assess your students' skill levels, strengths, learning needs, and any age restrictions that are applied to electronic books, gadgets, or apps. It's also worth considering the purpose of the tool. For example, visual aids are useful when supporting verbal communication. Electronic games and apps are useful to get students to follow prompts and directions.

Before using aided AAC systems like technological software, consult with a speech-language pathologist or special education teacher to get feedback on which software to use and how to support your students' diverse learning needs.

Implementing Visual Supports

Accessible learning is fundamental to providing a supportive classroom environment for students with ASD. Many students on the spectrum have difficulty understanding the nuances of language, including figures of speech, tone of voice, idioms, and sarcasm. The role of visual supports is to supplement verbal communication and make messages clearer. They provide visual cues, reminders, and illustrations of what students have been taught. There are various things that students can learn and remember through utilizing visual supports, such as:

- school and classroom rules

- daily routines, rosters, and calendars

- steps to perform specific activities or assignments

- tips on how to strike conversations with classmates

- memory recall (e.g., through reading labels like those on specific storage boxes or labels specifying different zones in the classroom)

Below is a list of the different visual supports you can use in your classroom.

Emotions Charts

Younger students who are still learning to identify and label their emotions may benefit from having access to an emotions chart. These charts illustrate different emotions through emojis and help students expand their vocabulary and ability to recognize a range of emotions. You can use the charts as part of the learning experience by designing lessons around them.

Visual Schedules

Visual schedules assist students with a range of executive function skills such as planning, time management, and organization. Moreover, they help anxious students anticipate upcoming transitions so that they aren't caught off guard when they come. Changes to schedules can also be visually depicted to remind students of adjustments they will need to make. For example, the amended deadline for a task might be written down on a notice board to allow students the time to make the necessary adjustments.

Choice Boards

Choice boards improve students' decision-making abilities by showing them the options they have available at any given time. Instead of verbalizing the choices that students have (which can be confusing to students with attention and memory problems), you can show them two pictures and ask them to choose an option. This strategy works best for choices involving the sequence of tasks (e.g., completing a reading or writing task first), food options during lunchtime, ideas on how to spend unstructured time, and ideas on craft activities.

Countdown Timers

It can be difficult for students with ASD to stay on top of time when completing tasks. Countdown timers are visual aids that show students how much time they have remaining. This reminder can help them manage their time when working on assignments and prevent meltdowns when their time is up. Another way to use countdown timers is to help students transition from one activity to another. Managing change can be challenging for students with ASD, especially when they are hyperfocused on their special interests. Having a countdown timer in place helps students regulate their emotions and prepare for what's to come.

Visual Positive Reinforcement Systems

Encouragement with words won't work for some students. Students with ASD are visual learners, meaning that they need to see that they are making progress rather than being told so. Visual positive reinforcement systems display goals and milestones that students need to achieve to meet the standards set by the teacher. For example, on a rewards chart, students can see what type of behaviors they are expected to perform (and how often they need to perform them) to earn tokens or gain access to certain toys and rewards. This creates an incentive for them to modify their behaviors and practice desired behaviors consistently until they become habits. As a bonus, having achievements publicly displayed in the classroom can reinforce good behaviors and make students feel proud of themselves.

Visual supports can be bought in stationery shops or from teachers' resource websites. If you are planning on making your own visual supports, remember to make them portable (or include a digital version). Ensure that they are durable to prevent wear and tear and visually appealing without being cluttered. Conduct A/B testing of two similar visual aids with your students before putting them up on the wall or using them during activities.

Group Activity: AAC System Exploration

Bring teachers together in your classroom and set up stations with different types of aided AAC tools (e.g., picture boards and educational apps). Include descriptions and how-to steps for using the AAC tools. Encourage teachers to walk to the different stations and learn more about how to use and implement the tools in the classroom. Once the walk-throughs have been done, sit down as a group and discuss the benefits and challenges of each tool, as well as innovative ways to integrate them into instruction.

Individual Activity: Visual Supports Plan

Develop a plan for using visual supports in daily classroom routines and activities. Identify specific instances when visual supports could be beneficial for students (e.g., preparing for transitions, enhancing social skills, or reminders for assignment submissions). Brainstorm ideas for creating and implementing these supports and create mock-up designs to envision how they would look. Test the mock-ups with your students before formalizing and putting them into practice.

In this chapter, we have discussed the importance of enhancing students' receptive language skills so that they can confidently understand and use information for their benefit. Let's cross over to the next chapter and explore strategies for communicating with nonverbal students or students with limited speech and language range.

Chapter 10:

Understanding and Responding to Nonverbal Communication

Not being able to speak is not the same as not having anything to say.
–Rosemary Crossley

Autism and Body Language

Students who grow up with developmental delays and sensory processing issues don't have a sense of what "acting normal" looks like. Everything they do falls outside the social norm. This factor alone can lead to unintentional miscommunication, especially when there is a lack of understanding of autism and how it manifests. In this chapter, we will explore how students on the spectrum use nonverbal communication—body language in particular—to convey messages about what they are thinking and feeling.

Students with ASD use their bodies as sensory machines. They are constantly sensing and feeling their way through the world, picking up on subtle and strong signals from their environments. They are sensitive to sudden changes that occur around them and their temperaments can change rapidly depending on the new sensory experiences they are picking up.

Sometimes, students with ASD may appear to be unapproachable, emotionless, or disinterested in social interactions. For instance, they may be quiet and stare at others in a group setting or may show no facial expressions when others are speaking. This is often mistaken as a lack of empathy; however, the truth is that it has more to do with self-regulation, in particular, regulating their internal experiences. Unlike typical students who could listen to a sad story, empathize, and move on to another subject, autistic students embody the story, feel the pain of the other person, and experience symptoms of stress. This is because they are highly sensitive and cannot regulate how much they absorb from others. Zoning out during social interactions is their way of maintaining a sense of control over their bodies and preventing overstimulation.

Students with ASD are constantly observing their environments for new stimuli, whether they are conscious of it or not. At the same time, they have coping mechanisms in place like stimming that allow them to regulate their sensory nervous systems. It's only when they feel safe and grounded that they can come out of their comfort zones. Until then, they prefer to be a wallflower.

This can also explain why students with ASD have a strong resistance to change and may take months to learn new routines or accept life transitions. Sudden and unexpected changes threaten their sense of safety and cause an immense amount of stress, which leads to overstimulation. To regain a sense of normalcy, students may use repetitive movements and behaviors to focus and feel calm. When you notice students bouncing on the spot, biting their nails, sucking their thumbs, tapping their pens, or repeating certain actions obsessively, they may be feeling anxious and doing their best to self-regulate.

How to Decode the Body Language of Students With ASD

The body language of students with ASD looks different from that of other students. It can take months and even years to understand what your students need or what they are feeling without them using spoken language. With that said, the process of decoding your students' body language can be rewarding, because it enables you to build stronger bonds with them.

Below is a short list of body language signs and what they mean for students with ASD. Keep a journal and make note of other cues that you notice to keep track of patterns of nonverbal communication behaviors. Note that not all body language will have different meanings. For example, a thumbs-up for a typical student means the same as a thumbs-up for an autistic student.

Blank Facial Expression

A blank facial expression means that the student is focused intensely on something. It could be a recurring thought, physical symptoms like stomach cramps, or specific details on someone's face. A blank stare during stressful situations could be a coping mechanism for managing strong impulses.

Delayed Reaction Time

When students seem almost frozen in time, it isn't because they are distracted or disengaged. Due to sensory processing issues, they may desire to make certain gestures or take certain actions, but their body is out of sync with the speed at which they can process sensory information. Don't be alarmed if they get back to you an hour after you asked them a question or if they mention that they are frustrated about something that happened a week ago.

Stimming

Stimming, as mentioned before, is a series of repetitive actions that enable autistic students to regulate their emotions. Some students may hide their stimming behaviors due to the stigma around them. For example, a high school student may be ashamed of sucking their thumb because it is seen as childish. Some stimming behaviors can be disruptive or harmful, such as banging the head on a desk, running in the classroom, or flapping hands in tight spaces. Help students replace those stims with safer options, but continue to encourage them to stim.

Eye Contact

Students with ASD find eye contact very uncomfortable. Many of them will avoid it if possible. Instead of pointing out their lack of eye contact, let them decide how often to look at you. Make sure that your face is relaxed and that you appear calm and friendly to help them feel at ease talking with you. If eye contact is a serious challenge for some students, consider adjusting learning expectations to accommodate them. For example, you wouldn't mark them down on their speeches or presentations for a lack of eye contact.

Proprioception Challenges

It is common for students with ASD to experience proprioception challenges, meaning that they don't receive signals helping them to coordinate and use different body parts. This may cause them to stomp or drag their feet when walking, use objects with extra force, or walk with poor posture due to having trouble engaging some muscle groups. Someone unaware of these challenges may mislabel these symptoms as signs of aggression, laziness, or carelessness.

Strategies for Teaching the Importance of Personal Space

Personal space can be a tricky concept for students with ASD to grapple with because of their proprioception challenges. They may not be aware when they are standing too close or touching someone forcefully. However, personal space issues are a common problem for all children, so this is a skill that the whole class ought to learn and practice. To avoid negative feedback and crossing physical boundaries, teach your students how to respect others' personal space. Below are some strategies that you can practice.

Use Social Stories About Personal Space

Create or find stories that address personal space issues. If you are creating them, use everyday scenarios where students would need to be mindful of those around them, such as lining up, during playtime, on the bench, or during group activities. The stories should show students what respecting one's personal space looks like and social cues that reveal that one is uncomfortable.

Use Visual Cues to Demarcate Space Boundaries

Visual cues can help students determine where to stand or sit, or how much space to leave between them and someone else. You can have students sit inside Hula-Hoops, sit on colored square patches on the floor, or measure the appropriate distance between them and others using arm length as a measuring stick.

Teach Social Cues to Understand Body Language

Go through some of the social cues that indicate that someone might be feeling uncomfortable due to invading their personal bubble. For example, students can look out for the following behaviors:

- moving the face or body away

- moving the chair or desk away

- crossing arms or legs

- putting a hand up with the palm facing out

- fidgeting or looking like they want to escape

Use role-playing and get the whole class involved when teaching social cues. You can even create visual aids to remind students of signs that they have invaded someone else's personal space.

Model Healthy Physical Boundaries

Show students what respecting personal space looks like by modeling the right behaviors in everyday interactions. For example, instead of hugging students, you can extend your hand to greet them, or when students insist on sitting on your lap, you can kindly ask them to sit on their square or designated spot. Remind them what standing too close looks like by saying things like "I forgot to stand an arm's length from you. Let me step back." Moreover, you can use specific phrases in your communication to teach students more about personal space. Examples of the phrases you can use include

- May I please have some space?

- You are standing too close.

- Could you please come closer?

Miss Harrison, a first-grade teacher, had concerns about her students who didn't understand personal space. They would stand extremely close to each other during lineup and other classroom activities and talk in each other's faces. One day, Miss Harrison came to class and decided to have a lesson centered around personal space. After defining and explaining the significance of personal space, she asked the students to get up from their seats and take a walk with her outside.

She divided them into pairs and told one team member, who would be the personal space invader, to stand on the far left side of the open field, and the other team member, who would demonstrate their personal space, to stand on the far right side. She introduced an exercise similar to the "Red, Yellow, Green Light" game. She instructed the students on the far left side of the field (the personal space invaders) to start walking forward toward their team members on the opposite side, who needed to yell "Yellow light!" or "Red light!" when their team members stood too close.

The students demonstrating personal space needed to assess for themselves what distance felt uncomfortable (i.e., warranting a yellow light) and what distance felt invasive (i.e., warranting a red light). The personal invaders needed to pause and assess what both uncomfortable and invasive distance looked like for their counterparts. Thereafter, the students would switch roles and repeat the process.

Miss Harrison carried out this exercise whenever she had free time. It allowed the students to get some fresh air and practice respecting personal space. The best part is that the "Red, Yellow, Green Light" phrase became popularly used in the classroom to indicate when peers were standing too close.

Group Activity: Nonverbal Communication Role-Play

Divide teachers into pairs and assign them a scenario involving body language expressed by students with ASD (e.g., lack of eye contact, stimming, or showing a blank face). Have them act out the scenarios, with one teacher taking the role of the student and the other responding as the teacher. Encourage both actors and the audience to reflect and discuss effective strategies for interpreting and responding to these nonverbal cues in a supportive way.

Individual Activity: Nonverbal Communication Reflection Journal

Use the following journal prompts to reflect on your own nonverbal communication skills. Focus on identifying strengths and areas for improvement when communicating nonverbal cues. End the exercise by setting goals for improving your nonverbal communication skills when interacting with your students. Consider the following prompts:

- Reflect on a recent conversation with a student where they appeared confused. Explore nonverbal cues that you could have offered to strengthen the delivery of your message.

- Describe a classroom situation where your nonverbal cues conveyed more information than words. Explain what was happening and the impact of your nonverbal communication.

- Describe a situation involving a student where changing your nonverbal cues during an interaction helped to bring a positive resolution or lead to a mutual understanding. What did you do well in that situation?

- Reflect on a time when inappropriate nonverbal cues during an exchange with a student made a situation worse. Consider how your nonverbal cues may have been perceived and how they negatively impacted the outcome.

- Describe a classroom situation that left you feeling speechless. Describe what you were feeling and how your body reacted. Assess whether you took the right actions at that moment and what you could've done better.

In this chapter, we discussed how nonverbal communication looks and feels for students with ASD. You now have a better understanding of how to interpret puzzling nonverbal cues that your students may display. We can proceed to the next chapter and look at effective solutions for developing literacy and language skills.

Chapter 11:

Building Language and Literacy Skills

My autism is not a deficiency. It is a different way of being. My mind is not flawed. It is complex.
–Dr. Lamar Hardwick

Supporting Speech and Language Development

In Chapter 9, we discussed the impact of receptive language skill deficiencies on students with ASD. We noted that before students can feel confident articulating their thoughts and feelings, they must feel confident processing and interpreting information. In this chapter, we are going to look at the impact of poor expressive language skills, which is a challenge that some students may face. What they struggle with the most isn't so much as understanding instructions as with formulating speech and speaking fluently.

Speech and language development begins around the ages of 6–9 months and gradually improves as a child gets older. During each periodic checkup, the doctor will evaluate the milestones reached, like whether the baby can form syllables, imitate tone and vowel sounds, or formulate words. By the time a child turns 5, they know more than 2,500 words and can formulate coherent and grammatically correct sentences (Healthdirect Australia, n.d.).

It is normal for children to reach their developmental milestones at different times. However, living with autism can cause significant speech and language delays for some. There are many reasons why this happens, all of which point to ASD symptoms.

For instance, certain conditions must be met to develop speech and language skills. First and foremost, children must desire to speak. This desire is often seen in small children babbling unrecognizable sounds or imitating and following prompts when their caregivers make speech sounds. Secondly, developing speech and language skills requires an understanding of the social context and expected reactions when certain information is communicated. For example, when asked a direct yes or no question, children need to know how to respond.

Lastly, what makes using speech and language easier for children is understanding the mental representation of the message, such as the meaning of the words and what is being implied. Afterward, they can respond to what they have heard and understood using speech or nonverbal language.

You may have identified a few autistic students who have difficulties with one or all three components of formulating speech and language. They might show a lack of interest in using words to speak, an inability to react appropriately to social contexts using words, or a lack of understanding of the meaning behind words and messages. These factors can cause speech and language delays that can either be temporary or lead to a diagnosis of related disorders.

Symptoms of severe speech and language challenges you will need to look out for include

- not speaking at all

- inability to express basic needs and wants

- using foreign words or language that you don't understand

- not responding to questions or reacting to commands

- repeating words or phrases spoken by the people around them

- using words or phrases without any facial expression or variation in tone

- making unusual sounds like grunts or shrieks when attempting to speak

Keep in mind that some students may be bilingual or multilingual, which means that their speech and vocabulary range is vast and can sometimes be mixed in conversation. Speak to parents to find out more about the children's language history and whether they are open to exploring language training.

Speech therapy is the most commonly used method for improving speech and language skills. It is administered by a speech-language pathologist who is qualified to diagnose and treat a range of speech and language disorders. Before a student can start with the therapy, they will be taken through a formal assessment and asked questions about their family and medical history. Based on the results of the assessment, the speech-language pathologist will create a tailored treatment plan and work closely with parents (and sometimes educators) to help the student improve their speaking abilities.

The treatment plan will take into consideration certain factors such as the student's age, needs, and speech or language disorder. The techniques included in the treatment plan will also vary and may include things like:

- using AAC devices

- using visual supports

- echoing words

- prompting

- vocabulary expansion

- sentence expansion

- social stories and role-play

- articulation exercises

- turn-taking and conversation skills

What's great about these techniques is that they can be done at home and inside the classroom. With the support of parents and teachers and a carefully structured IEP plan (in most cases), students with speech and language disorders can improve their word knowledge, speech production, and conversational abilities. With that said, the earlier the interventions are initiated, the better the results.

Strategies for Enhancing Reading Comprehension

Speech and language challenges can affect students' reading comprehension skills. To understand written text, they must have an expansive vocabulary and know the meaning behind words, parts of speech, and figures of speech.

Students who lack the necessary receptive and expressive language skills may find it difficult to recognize words, decode text, identify language patterns, and construct sentences. Some may find it hard to make connections between what they are reading and the follow-up questions they are asked. This has to do with the lack of understanding of the role, meaning, and impact of the words and sentences.

As students reach higher grades, reading comprehension skills become more advanced. They are expected to form an understanding of the three levels of comprehension, which are

- **Literal comprehension:** The ability to understand what is being said or what is happening at face value. This may include identifying the main idea, facts, or sequence of events mentioned in the text. The literal level is the foundation level of reading comprehension that requires students to display basic cognitive skills.

- **Inferential comprehension:** The ability to make inferences or draw meaningful conclusions from the text. Before you can do this, you need to understand the main idea, facts, or sequence of events. The first level of reading comprehension deals with the "what" whereas the second level addresses the "why."

- **Evaluative comprehension:** The ability to analyze the text and look at the broader impact or implications of what is written. Evaluations are subjective; however, they are grounded in theory. In other words, students need to make connections between two separate pieces of information: the text, and the theory that supports it.

Teaching students with ASD how to decode text in this manner requires you to use a familiar approach that doesn't involve skills they already lack. For example, if a student doesn't understand the meaning of a word, it is not helpful to repeat the word, write it down, or include it in a sentence. They will simply gloss over it and attempt to understand the next word in the sentence. You would need to use strategies that students recognize and have practiced before, such as using pictures, animations, stories, and role-playing to help them understand the meaning of a word.

Below are a handful of ASD-friendly strategies that can enhance students' reading comprehension skills without complicating the process for them.

Use Visual Books or Boards

A picture can indeed tell a thousand words. Many students with ASD are visual learners, which means that they can retain information better when it is visually represented. The combination of seeing, hearing, and repeating information can enhance memory and help students learn words, sounds, emotions, and symbols.

Read With Students

Encourage students to read the text after you and imitate the tone, pitch, and sounds that you make. This is a great speech recognition and articulation exercise that allows students to learn new words, sentence structures, and the correct pronunciation. When reading with students, you can also use prompting by pointing a finger at certain words and waiting for them to say the word out loud.

Make Text Interesting

Students who lack reading comprehension skills may have negative feelings toward tasks of that nature. As a result, they could be discouraged from enhancing their skills. One of the ways to incentivize reading is to present text that students would be interested in reading. Include your students' special interests and favorite topics in reading comprehension exercises to keep them engaged.

Use AAC Devices

AAC devices offer an alternative approach to developing reading comprehension skills. Students are presented with information in a form that is easy for them to interact with. For example, audiobooks can help students follow along with the narrator and make associations between voice-generated sounds and written words. Older students can benefit from visual learning software that helps them map out information using graphic mind maps and draw meaningful conclusions. Another advantage of digital text is that it can be modified (i.e., changing the font size, spacing, or color contrast) to accommodate students' learning needs.

Help Students Connect the Dots

Teach students how to make a connection between what they already know and what they are currently reading. This link can be made by asking reflection questions that enable students to think back to their own experiences or tap into their existing inventory of skills and knowledge.

Developing reading comprehension skills takes time and reinforcement. It isn't enough for students to only be exposed to these skills at school. Encourage parents to get their children into the habit of reading by buying books to read at home and regularly reading to them (or with them).

Overcoming Writing Challenges

We have spoken about the reading challenges that students with ASD can encounter, but what about their writing challenges? Research has found that autistic people have trouble with handwriting due to executive function and motor coordination deficiencies (Asaro–Saddler, 2013). Good handwriting is an important skill for students to learn and master because it enables them to display their knowledge and allows you, as the teacher, to evaluate their level of understanding.

Let's go over some strategies that you can practice in the classroom to help students improve their writing abilities.

Practice Fine Motor Skills

Fine motor skills teach students how to coordinate their eyes, hands, and fingers, and how to make the appropriate motions when writing. Classroom exercises that can help students improve their fine motor skills include squeezing a stress ball, using a pair of tweezers to pick up small objects, doing tracing and drawing activities, and offering students the option of using adaptive writing tools and grips.

Create an Environment Conducive to Writing

Students on the spectrum thrive in calm and supportive environments. Make sure that they are aware of upcoming writing tasks and can mentally prepare themselves in advance. It can be helpful to create a schedule and always place writing tasks at the same time to make them more predictable. Using visual supports like charts and checklists can also assist students in remembering the steps of the writing process. Additionally, you can assign individual storage bins or folders to help students stay organized so they can easily access their written assignments.

Make Accommodations

When you have identified students with writing challenges, it is perfectly okay to make special accommodations such as adjusting instructions to address their learning needs. For example, you might change writing instructions or activities slightly to allow students to engage without being held back by their writing deficits. You could also provide visual aids to demonstrate how students should organize their thoughts or structure their writing. Some students may need additional time to complete assignments, while others could benefit from using assistive technologies like speech-to-text devices.

Promote Self-Expression

Some students with ASD need a lot of motivation to focus during writing tasks. Incorporate writing tasks that give students the freedom to write about anything they want. For example, you could present a prompt and ask them to write a complete story with a plot, setting, and characters. Additionally, you can introduce students to fun writing activities like having pen pals, journaling, and goal-setting. This allows them to be creative and gravitate to topics they are passionate about or write in their own style, using vocabulary they are comfortable with. Promoting self-expression in writing allows students to develop a love for writing and enhances their writing skills.

Group Activity: Literacy Activity Planning Session

Collaborate with other teachers to design fun and interactive literacy activities that engage students' interests while addressing their reading and writing challenges. Some of the ideas that you can put forward include having interactive read-aloud sessions, theme-based spelling tests, and daily writing prompts.

Individual Activity: Language-Focused Lesson Plan

Design and implement a language-focused lesson tailored to meet the needs of students with ASD while being inclusive of the rest of the class. Choose one or two language skills to address and reflect on how you can use AAC systems to strengthen understanding. Host the lesson and gather student feedback through a quiz or questionnaire at the end of the lesson. Make adjustments to future lessons based on observed outcomes and student progress.

In this chapter, you have been taken through the common literacy challenges faced by students with ASD and meaningful ways to address them. Let's proceed to the next chapter and explore ways that you can promote independent learning among students with ASD.

Chapter 12:

Promoting Independence and Task Completion

Autism is not a puzzle, nor a disease. Autism is a challenge, but certainly not a devastating one.
–Trisha Van Berkel

Why Is Teaching Independence So Important?

As students get older, they desire to have more autonomy over their learning and complete tasks without the supervision of a teacher. However, what students don't understand is that certain skills are necessary when developing independence, and unless those skills are learned first, they will need ongoing support and monitoring in completing tasks.

Students on the spectrum require a lot of prompting and guidance when completing tasks. Younger students may appreciate the hand-holding; however, older students may find it overwhelming. Like their peers, they want to feel a sense of competence and achievement in being left to make decisions and solve problems independently. However, they may struggle with listening, attention, and memory skills—all the skills that are needed to enable them to work independently.

It is crucial to start as young as possible in order to teach your students how to work and learn independently. Not only is this good for their self-esteem, but it can also help them manage academic challenges as they advance to higher grades. Some of the skills that students with ASD need support with include the following points:

- **Organization:** Independent students know how to manage their time wisely and develop plans for staying on track with school demands. Organizational skills can be taught by having your students clean up after themselves, make use of storage bins and folders, set goals and milestones, and create their own study and homework timetables.

- **Self-Monitoring:** The biggest barriers to achieving focus are frequent distractions and sensory triggers that interfere with their progress. Self-monitoring is a proactive technique that teaches students how to regulate their behaviors in social settings. It can reduce distractibility by encouraging students to identify triggers (e.g., sensory overwhelm) and take action to regulate their bodies and redirect their attention to the tasks at hand.

- **Prioritization:** Some students with ASD may have a difficult time going through a long list of tasks. If they were to have it their way, they would only complete the tasks they prefer and leave the rest. Students need to learn how to differentiate between urgent, important, and unimportant tasks. For instance, tasks that have deadlines approaching soon must be completed before tasks that don't have deadlines or tasks that won't be graded.

How to Implement Work Systems to Encourage Independence

A work system is an instructional method used to help students take ownership of their learning. Tasks and activities are given with as much information as required to help students know what steps to take and what achieving success looks like. Four important pieces of information need to be communicated to students:

- Clear and actionable details of the tasks that students need to follow.

- Clear indications of the number of tasks students are required to complete.

- Criteria for success and what the final results should look like (and cues to know when they have completed the tasks or steps).

- Actions to be taken when students have completed the assignments (and indicating the next scheduled tasks to be completed).

Students who use work systems are encouraged to solve problems related to tasks using the information they have been given. Essentially, before raising their hands to ask questions, they are required to carefully read their instructions again and figure out what they need to do without being prompted by the teacher. Since work systems are highly organized and structured, they teach students how to work systematically, from top to bottom, left to right. Before working on tasks and activities, students understand their starting point and the steps they will need to perform to reach the finish line.

Here are additional tips that can help you set up work systems in your classroom:

- Provide all of the necessary tools and materials students will need to perform an activity. Clear their desks of other supplies to avoid confusion.

- Use work systems in different classroom contexts (i.e., not solely for academic work) to reinforce planning and organizational skills. For instance, you can implement work systems for lining up, lunchtime, classroom meetings, and going on field trips).

- In situations where you need to prompt students, use nonverbal prompting (e.g., nodding your head or pointing to words or pictures) to avoid saying too much and playing an active role in helping students complete their tasks.

- Create portable work systems for students to take outside of the classroom. This can be beneficial for students who need support in social settings, such as remembering conversational skills.

Teaching Time Management Skills

Students who lack time management skills may struggle with pacing themselves when completing tasks, adhering to assignment deadlines, and following routines and schedules. ASD symptoms like poor working memory, attention deficits, and the lack of time perception (i.e., the inability to perceive time in concrete and tangible ways) can interfere with students' ability to manage their time wisely.

The benefit of teaching students time management skills is that they can set and execute goals and enjoy more autonomy over their work process. Outside of the classroom, time management can help them manage extracurricular activities, improve their study skills, and prepare for college or employment responsibilities. The following are effective strategies that you can practice with your students to improve their time management skills.

Create Visual Schedules

Students who lack time perception may have difficulty understanding and tracking time. For instance, they underestimate how much time it would take to complete tasks and have trouble interpreting the sequence of events, such as what will take place in an hour's time or for a submission due two days from now.

Visual schedules like timetables can help students make sense of time in a tangible way. They can see the breakdown of their day and put things into perspective. For example, they can see what will happen now versus what will happen after recess.

When creating visual schedules, make sure that you include pictures of activities next to the time stamps to help visual learners understand the task expectations.

Use Timers

Timers are a great way to make the concept of time concrete. Students can periodically look at the countdown on the timer to see how much time they have remaining. Timers can also cue students to focus for a certain amount of time. After the countdown has finished, allow students to take a movement break before sitting down to begin the next activity. You can also encourage students to wear a digital wristwatch to school (if the school permits) so that they can get alerts whenever it is time to do something.

Encourage To-Do Lists

Teach students how to create simple to-do lists to remember the tasks they have to complete before the end of the day. Show them how to order tasks from the most to the least important. Older students can create more detailed to-do lists that include time estimations, priority status, and targeted completion dates for each task. Remind students to check off completed tasks on their list. This additional step gives them a sense of achievement and reinforces positive behaviors.

Turn Students Into Time Detectives

Make time management fun by presenting a challenge. Before students begin a task, ask them to take out a piece of paper and write down an estimate of how much time they will need to complete it, then calculate how much time it actually takes using a timer. They can use the classroom timer or their own wristwatches for this part. In the end, they get to see how accurate their time estimations are. Some might overestimate the time they will need, while others might underestimate it. Over time, their predictions will become more accurate.

The purpose of time management skills is to make students' lives more organized and predictable, which can lead to less anxiety around academic performance. They can also feel proud of themselves knowing that they can adhere to timeframes and deadlines.

Encouraging Self-Advocacy

Self-advocacy refers to standing up for yourself. It involves sharing your thoughts, expressing needs, and setting boundaries with others. Since students with ASD face many challenges at school, they need to be empowered to communicate their needs, ask for help, and voice their concerns, if they have any. This would allow them to get support from teachers and peers and feel confident in who they are.

Below are some skills you can practice in the classroom to promote self-advocacy.

Identity Exploration

Help students learn more about themselves through identity-building tasks. Get them to write, read, or speak about their strengths, interests, skills, abilities, and cultural backgrounds. Another way to explore identity is to encourage subjectivity. For instance, during classroom discussions, you might ask students to share their personal opinions, past experiences, or preferences.

Decision-Making

Whenever possible, allow students to make decisions related to their activities or daily routines. Give them options to decide which tasks to complete first, which games to play, or which books to read. Include an aspect of self-reflection by asking students the motivations behind their options. For example, you might ask, "Why have you chosen to read this book over the other one?" Reflection questions allow students to think about why certain things are important to them.

Goal-Setting

Instead of setting goals for your students, let them take the lead and set goals that are meaningful to them. Of course, you will need to facilitate these sessions by helping them organize their thoughts and put together a realistic plan. You can also choose to start goal-setting sessions by sharing performance or behavioral feedback with your students and then working together to create a visual milestone ladder that represents the steps required to achieve their goals. Meet regularly with students to discuss progress and adjust milestones when necessary.

Confidence Building

Confidence is one of the drivers of self-advocacy. Confident students can share their thoughts and feelings without fear of judgment. They also have a strong conviction in who they are and what they need in order to feel safe and comfortable at school.

A great way to help students build confidence is through role-playing. This technique teaches students how to deal with real-life situations by going through scripts and practicing taking on different roles. Over time, students develop the skills, knowledge, and language to express their needs and overcome their fears.

Personal Boundaries

Students with ASD need to know that it is important to set limits with others. They are not obliged to say yes to every request or accept mistreatment from their peers. Teach students about personal boundaries and why they are important. Go through the different types of boundaries (e.g., physical, emotional, mental, material) and provide simple scripts they can use to set boundaries with others. You can also teach students about their rights such as the right to privacy about their diagnosis, and how to assess when their rights or boundaries have been violated.

When teaching self-advocacy, encourage students to communicate using methods that feel comfortable for them. Some students might prefer to set boundaries using nonverbal cues like shaking their heads or making certain sounds when they are uncomfortable. Other students might prefer to express their needs by pointing to objects or pictures. You could also have some students who are better at written communication than verbal communication, so writing letters and journaling can be effective ways for them to share their thoughts.

Group Activity: Time Management Simulation

Divide teachers into groups and give them typical classroom scenarios where time management is crucial. Teachers must step into the shoes of their students and brainstorm strategies to effectively manage time and prioritize tasks within the given scenarios. Moreover, teachers must take into consideration the impact of various ASD symptoms and how these can cause difficulties for students. Afterward, groups can share their strategies and discuss which ones they found most effective.

Individual Activity: Time Management Reflection

Reflect on your current time management practices in the classroom. Identify what you are good at and what you can improve. Based on this analysis, develop an action plan outlining specific strategies you can implement in the classroom to enhance your students' time management skills, such as utilizing visual timers or creating structured schedules.

In this chapter, we discussed the importance of helping students develop independence and stand up for themselves. These two skills—independence and self-advocacy—can help students build competence and confidence in themselves and their ability to succeed at school.

We have now completed the third part of the book, which focuses on adopting ASD-friendly communication in the classroom. We can now proceed to the fourth and final part of the book and discuss strategies to manage ASD at different education levels.

PART 4:

Supportive Classroom Strategies for Students at Different Education Levels

Chapter 13:

ASD-Friendly Strategies for Elementary School

Everybody is a genius. But if you judge a fish by its ability to climb a tree, it will live its whole life believing that it is stupid.
—Albert Einstein

Creating Structured Classrooms

Like adults, elementary students need structure to feel in control and know what to expect throughout the day. For autistic students who fear change and have difficulty managing transitions, having structure enables them to feel safe and comfortable in their classroom.

The Division Treatment and Education of Autistic and related Communication-handicapped Children (TEACCH) program is a nationwide autism treatment model that creates teaching strategies to accommodate the needs of students on the spectrum (Hume & Indiana Resource Center for Autism, n.d.-b). One of the strategies promoted in the program is called Structured Teaching, which consists of a set of techniques to create a structured classroom setting. While these strategies are geared toward understanding and addressing ASD challenges, they can benefit all students in the classroom.

Structured Teaching outlines five elements that emphasize the importance of predictable classroom structure. These five elements are normally depicted in a pyramid to show how they build upon each other. Below is a breakdown of two elements—physical structure and predictable schedules—and an overview of how to integrate them into your classroom setting.

Physical Structure

Every classroom has a physical structure, that is, a specific layout and organization done to the space. Being intentional about the physical structure of your classroom can enhance learning and minimize distractions and sensory triggers. Students can also feel comfortable navigating the classroom when they understand how to use the space and what activities occur in each zone.

Every section of your classroom must have a clear purpose so that students are aware of how to modify their behaviors in that space. In other words, these clearly defined sections serve as cues to remind students of what is expected of them.

Boundaries can also be communicated through oral, written, and visual language. For example, you can instruct students on what they can or cannot do when seated at their desks or create a poster with a set of classroom rules to reinforce physical boundaries.

Additionally, you can set up an organizational system and teach students how to use it. For example, you can create storage locations for specific tasks and assignments and personal belongings like school bags, and an easy-to-follow routine for submitting assignments (e.g., have students drop their assignments into a submission box). You can also assign students small jobs around the classroom so they can help you minimize physical and visual clutter.

Predictable Schedules

Learning in a predictable classroom environment feels less stressful for students because they understand what to do and what comes next. Overcommunication is encouraged when preparing and sharing instructions. Information shouldn't solely be communicated through verbal instructions, but through visual instructions, too. The benefit of creating visual schedules is that students get to see the sequence of activities, even if they cannot conceptualize them in their minds. Some students may find visual scheduling easier to access and understand than receiving direct instructions. In the end, they feel less confused about what they need to do, and this can reduce challenging behaviors.

Routines are tangible schedules that students interact with. They serve multiple purposes, but two of the main ones are to make daily activities predictable and to help students manage transitions. Get students involved in setting up their routines to increase their cooperation and engagement. Create room for variances in the routines, such as opting to work outdoors instead of inside the classroom in order to teach students with ASD how to adapt to change without feeling overwhelmed.

Utilizing Special Interests in Learning

A quirky characteristic of autism that affects over 90% of children and adults with Asperger's syndrome is having special interests (Vrana, n.d.). Special interests refer to an intense fascination or obsession with particular interests, objects, or subjects.

Many of us have favorite topics or passions that we like to speak about from time to time. However, for students with ASD, special interests take on a more serious nature. Their fascination or obsession with certain things consumes their minds and serves as a comparative reference point to interactions experienced in the classroom. Thus, leveraging special interests can be an effective teaching method to get students to build skills and engage with the learning materials.

To adopt special interests into activities and lessons, you will need to learn about your students' special interest areas. This could range from 100-piece puzzles to fictional superheroes. Note that the way that students engage with their special interests will vary too. Some might be interested in collecting facts about their special interests (e.g. learning the names of all the US presidents since the beginning of democracy) while others might be interested in showing empathy for their special interests (e.g., rescuing and caring for cats).

There is often a stigma around special interests, which makes students ashamed of expressing what they are. For example, a student might be fascinated by something that their peers find childish or strange. Creating a culture of acceptance in the classroom can allow students to feel safe talking about their special interests without the fear of judgment. Acceptance can be translated into classwork by incorporating a diverse range of special interests in classroom activities to expose students to topics they haven't heard about or delved into deeply. Some of the ways that you can teach using special interests include

- using special interests for counting, teaching social skills, or comparing the similarities and differences between things

- allowing students to engage with technology that explores their special interests, such as visiting specific websites, playing online games, watching specific videos, or listening to specific music

- creating projects or assignments centered around special interests (ensure that you include a case study, description, or background information about the special interest area to help students who may not be familiar with it)

Engaging in special interests can be fun; however, clear boundaries need to be put in place to regulate how much access students have to them. Sometimes special interests can take students down a rabbit hole and expose them to inappropriate information. Other times special interests distract students from other important school tasks.

Boundaries such as blocking certain apps or websites from students' devices can be automatic. They can also be communicated every time students ask to access their special interests. For example, you can have rules about when it is appropriate for students to explore their special interests. Appropriate times could be during unstructured classroom time, after submitting classwork, or during recess.

When communicating special interest boundaries, avoid being direct and saying "no," as this could be triggering for some autistic students. Instead, tell students when they will be allowed to access their special interests. For example, you might say, "When you have completed your science experiment, you are welcome to play with your figurines."

Checklist: Creating Sensory-Friendly Learning Spaces

Earlier in the chapter, we explored the importance of creating a structured environment in the classroom. A special consideration that you will need to make for young students on the spectrum is minimizing sensory distractions that would cause anxiety and unwanted behaviors. Below is a checklist that can help you transform your classroom and create a sensory-friendly and supportive space for students.

Provision	Well developed	Partly developed	Not yet developed
Visual schedules are put on display in the classroom.			
Students are given enough visual cues to support smooth transitions between tasks.			
Clear signposts and labels are placed around the classroom to			

Provision	Well developed	Partly developed	Not yet developed
demarcate zones.			
Learning materials and resources are labeled and color-coded.			
An appropriate seating layout has been done to minimize distractions.			
A low arousal or "quiet zone" has been created in the classroom.			
Multisensory activities are provided to accommodate students' learning styles.			
Classroom activities and rewards incorporate special interests.			
Students are given choices to encourage independence and			

Provision	Well developed	Partly developed	Not yet developed
decision-making.			
Consistent routines are followed to create a predictable environment.			
Clear social and classroom rules are communicated through spoken, visual, and written language.			
A structured approach is taken when ensuring that students have something to do during unstructured time.			
Sensory distractions such as bright lights or loud noises are limited in the classroom.			
A behavioral management system has been created to manage sensory overload and challenging			

Provision	Well developed	Partly developed	Not yet developed
behaviors.			

Elementary school students thrive in a structured and engaging classroom environment. Some of the ways to appeal to their learning needs are to adjust the physical structure to accommodate their sensory needs and include their special interests as part of the learning experience.

Now that you are familiar with the needs of students in elementary school, let's cross over to the next chapter and learn about specific strategies for managing ASD in middle school.

Chapter 14:

ASD-Friendly Strategies for Middle School

Sometimes it is the people no one can imagine anything of who do the things no one can imagine.
–Alan Turing

Transitioning to Middle School

The transition from elementary school to middle school can be difficult for students with ASD due to the significant changes in routines and the school demands that come with it. Even students who are deemed as having low support needs will struggle to mentally and emotionally cope with the changes.

This can impact their learning in different ways. For instance, students could have unexplained meltdowns, conflicts with their peers, social anxiety, or trouble concentrating in class.

Transition planning is crucial to ensure that students feel prepared for what lies ahead in middle school. This plan is designed by elementary school teachers in collaboration with parents. The purpose of the plan is to identify the social and academic skills that students will need for grades 5–8 and teach them the basics at least two years before they transition to middle school. In other words, transition preparations could start from as early as third grade. Starting this early is necessary for autistic students who tend to have developmental delays.

Parents whose students are on an IEP will need to schedule a meeting with the IEP team before their children enter middle school. Some of the items to discuss at the meeting can include reassessing the child's social and academic needs, evaluating the effectiveness of the services and interventions for middle school, and making special accommodations to support the child's learning needs.

There are three ways to identify students who are having trouble managing the transition into middle school:

- Students perform repetitive behaviors that interfere with their ability to learn or engage with their peers.

- Students are unresponsive to instructions or guidance offered by the teacher (e.g., they might pretend to not hear what the teacher is saying).

- Students exhibit challenging behaviors such as throwing objects, prolonged tantrums, verbal aggression, withdrawal, or self-injury.

Having preventative strategies put in place can make managing transitions a lot easier. Think about the small adjustments you can make to your teaching practice to lower students' anxiety around social and academic expectations. Here are a few suggestions:

- **Plan lessons ahead of time:** The more organized you are, the calmer students will be. Get into the habit of planning lessons and activities ahead of time to allow you to create detailed schedules and instructional material as well as to be able to source the required tools and supplies.

- **Be consistent with your timetable:** Create a timetable that consists of the subjects or tasks that students will complete daily. Provide students with printed or digital copies of the timetable to ensure they know the sequence of events throughout the day. If there will be any changes to the timetable, communicate them at the start of the day to give students time to adjust.

- **Have a contingency plan for challenging behavior:** Despite your best efforts to create a predictable classroom environment, some students may find managing transitions difficult. Have a plan put in place to identify and address challenging behavior. The plan could include self-regulation and PBS strategies to de-escalate the situation.

- **Include sensory breaks into your routine:** Students with ASD can become easily overwhelmed when they have been sitting down for too long, focusing for too long, or witnessing the commotion in the classroom. Sensory breaks provide students a chance to get up from their seats and move around. Offer suggestions on the activities students can engage with during their sensory breaks, such as going to the restroom, drinking water, spending time in the quiet zone, or taking deep breaths.

Another way to plan for transitions is to break them down into three phases: the preparation, transition, and end phase. For instance, before giving students instructions to switch between tasks, you can give them a warning of the upcoming change. Your warning should have a visual and auditory element. For example, you can place a countdown timer in the front of the classroom for students to look at. On top of this, you can get everyone's attention and make an announcement.

When it's time to make the transition, make sure students know what they are expected to do. Provide simple directions that they can follow, such as, "Let's close our English books and put them away." You can also play music during transitions to remind students that it's time to move on to something different. Make sure that you use the same consistent strategies to help students manage transitions.

The end phase happens after the transition occurs. What's important about his phase is to offer positive reinforcement so that students are motivated to repeat the same desirable behaviors for the next transition. Give sincere and targeted feedback about what you saw and appreciated. For example, you might thank your students for cleaning up their stations and lining up immediately after being instructed, for submitting their assignments on time, returning to class on time after recess, and so on. Focus on acknowledging good efforts rather than perfection.

Managing Homework and Assignments

It's normal for homework demands to pick up during middle school. Students who need a lot of guidance and hand-holding may struggle to complete homework, especially when they are not getting adequate support at home. They might refuse to do homework or submit assignments that are poorly written or half-completed.

On a surface level, it might seem that students are being defiant by not completing their homework or assignments. However, as with the case of autistic students, there could be other factors at play which make the process difficult, such as

- **Rigid thinking patterns:** Students may have trouble adjusting to carrying out schoolwork at home. In their minds, they see home as being a time to relax and school as being a time to work. Sitting down to complete homework feels unfair to them because they have spent the whole day at school working.

- **Sensory stress:** Managing to get through a school day without any hiccups or acted-upon triggers is an achievement for students on the spectrum. When they get home, they desire to unwind and focus on activities that feel pleasurable.

- **Comprehension:** Students with ASD can be discouraged easily when they don't understand the instructions given to them. Sometimes, the reason for not completing homework is due to a lack of understanding and problem-solving.

- **Executive function skills:** Some homework tasks and assignments may require students to demonstrate executive function skills like planning, memorization, or critical thinking. Students who lack these skills may struggle to complete the work independently.

- **Fear of failure:** Students who are not doing well at school may feel inadequate and may therefore avoid completing homework tasks that could expose their weaknesses. Some students who struggle with low self-esteem might allow limiting beliefs to get in the way of their academic performance. These limiting beliefs become self-fulfilling prophecies when students are unable to push themselves to work hard.

Fortunately, there are some strategies that you can practice to lower students' resistance when it comes to completing homework and other assignments. Here are some that you can consider.

Define the Purpose

Motivation is a big driver for autistic students. For them to take homework assignments seriously, they need to understand the purpose behind what they are doing. They need to see how their efforts will help them achieve the desired outcomes. For example, you can create goals and objectives for homework assignments or connect them to classroom topics and activities to help students understand why they matter.

Start Homework at School

If possible, give students time toward the end of the day to start working on their homework tasks. Getting a head start at school allows them to ask questions and receive the support of their teacher. Furthermore, reducing their workload while at school can relieve stress when they get home and make finishing their tasks feel less daunting.

Experiment With Peak Performance

Advise parents to test when their children are most productive at different times of the day. Some children may have a lot of energy after school; others may feel tired and prefer to take a nap before getting started with homework. Children who are early risers may feel energized in the mornings. Doing homework before school could feel more convenient for them. Children who are night owls may concentrate better in the evenings when the house is quieter and there are minimal distractions.

Have a One-on-One Meeting

Sit down with students and their parents to discuss the challenges they may be facing when completing homework. Note the concerns that students have and consider whether you can make special accommodations for them. If there are serious issues brought up that impact students' well-being, refer them to the school counselor for further support and evaluation.

Students who are on an IEP can request homework modifications due to ongoing frustrations and problems with completing tasks and assignments. Remember that modifications are different from adjustments. When you modify expectations, you are changing the content or instructions to accommodate students' needs. This implies that the academic standard can drop slightly, which can impact students in the long term. Nevertheless, examples of modifications that you can make to homework expectations include

- reducing the length of homework assignments for students

- allowing students to use speech-to-text devices when completing writing tasks

- offering students modified assignments that are graded differently from their peers

- exempting students from completing homework

- allowing students to receive excessive assistance from parents

- allowing students to use technology like homework apps to assist in completing tasks

You can also sit down with parents and discuss the option of hiring homework mentors or tutors. Homework mentors are people that children look up to such as older siblings or cousins. They play more of a supportive role in helping children stay on track with their school obligations. Tutors are authority figures who know children's academic needs. Their job is to teach and reinforce skills using age-appropriate methods and language. When selecting tutors, urge parents to choose people who have experience tutoring children with autism or other similar disabilities.

Middle school can be stressful for students on the spectrum because of the increase in school demands. By helping your students manage transitions and stay on track with completing their school assignments, they can quickly adapt to the new environment and stay motivated to work hard.

Now that you are familiar with the needs of students in middle school, let's cross over to the next chapter and learn about specific strategies for managing ASD in high school.

Chapter 15:

ASD-Friendly Strategies for High School

Showing kindness towards those who are different and embracing our imperfections as proof of our humanness is the remedy for fear.
–Emma Zurcher–Long

Executive Function Challenges in High School

High school exposes students to advanced skills and knowledge that requires critical thinking, reasoning, planning, and problem-solving. Students with ASD who may be experiencing executive function difficulties may feel incompetent and unprepared for the demands of high school.

Another challenge that adds to this is that students are expected to display a high level of independence at the high school level. For example, they may be expected to manage their time, create their own schedules, pay attention in class, remember details, and know how to decode advanced instructions. Students who cannot complete these skills find the pace of high school to be overwhelming, and they can quickly develop a negative perception of school or specific subjects.

One of the solutions to dealing with executive function challenges is to refer at-risk students for special education services so they can get access to services that can improve their learning experience. However, not all students will qualify for special education services. A more inclusive approach is to adjust your teaching practices in the classroom to improve executive function skills and encourage more engagement from students. Three models that you can adapt to your classroom settings are Universal Design for Learning (UDL), Positive Behavior Support (PBS), and the Developmental, Individual-differences, Relationship-based Model (DIR).

Universal Design for Learning

Universal Design for Learning (UDL) has been found to increase engagement and significantly improve learning outcomes for students with disabilities. The model advocates for inclusive and accessible learning that appeals to the strengths and needs of all students. Multiple formats, methods, and materials are used to present information to ensure that all students understand what is expected of them and can complete tasks with minimal difficulties. UDL assessments allow students to showcase their skills and knowledge in a manner that suits their learning styles. Students are graded on skills they have engaged with before rather than skills they are deficient in.

Positive Behavior Support

Positive Behavior Support (PBS) seeks to adjust environmental expectations for students demonstrating challenging behaviors. Similar to UDL, this is done to ensure that all students have access to learning. Before outlining interventions, the first step is to assess the executive function difficulties that students are encountering. Thereafter, you can brainstorm ways to redesign your teaching practices or classroom environment to enhance learning and decrease unwanted behaviors. For example, if you find that a student struggles to memorize information, you can teach them how to take notes in class, create to-do lists, set up homework schedules, and study for tests and exams.

Developmental, Individual-differences, Relationship-based Model

Developmental, Individual-differences, Relationship-based Model (DIR) is an individualized intervention that takes into consideration the learning needs of specific students. The process begins with understanding a student's academic strengths and weaknesses by observing how they absorb, process, and respond to information. Once this analysis has been done, teachers are tasked to work with parents and other support staff to build upon the student's strengths and address their challenges.

These three models prove that executive function skills can be enhanced in the classroom through individualized support and meaningful adjustments made to teaching methods. It is important to remind students who may be struggling with these skills that they can develop them with ongoing exposure and practice in a manner that is most suitable to their learning styles.

Teaching Social Problem-Solving

As students get older, it becomes crucial for them to learn how to navigate through various social interactions safely. Not only can this enhance their high school experience but it can also give them an advantage in a few years when they are navigating other social settings like college or the workplace. Social problem-solving skills teach students how to make informed decisions that might affect them and others. These skills foster healthy peer relationships and positive conflict management.

Social problem-solving involves several components, such as being able to

- define the problem or conflict

- brainstorm solutions

- choose the best solution and take action

- evaluate the outcomes

Learning social problem-solving skills allows students to learn and strengthen other social skills such as showing empathy, perspective-taking, negotiating, and decision-making. However, to gain all of these skills, students must double down on their problem-solving abilities. Without the knowledge of how to recognize, define, analyze, and resolve problems, students will feel lost and confused when encountering social dynamics or situations they have never come across before. You can introduce your students to the problem-solving process by showing them how to find, shape, and solve problems.

Step 1: Find the Problem

When students sense that something could be wrong in their environment, it prompts them to search for the problem. The problem could be internal, like being overstimulated or experiencing unwanted thoughts or emotions that are causing anxiety. It could also be external, like picking up negative body language from a peer.

Teach students to go through a set of questions to identify the problem. Questions may include:

- What am I thinking?
- What am I feeling?
- What am I seeing?
- What is missing?
- What do I need?

Step 2: Shape the Problem

The next step is to take a broad problem and narrow it down to something that can be solved. For example, instead of seeking to end world hunger, one might focus on feeding the homeless within the local community. Similarly, you can show students how to take an enormous problem that could be overwhelming for them and focus on a small piece that they can address in a manageable way. In most cases, shaping the problem encourages students to focus on adapting to the situation rather than seeking to fix or change the situation.

Step 3: Solve the Problem

Now that the problem has been identified and condensed, students can brainstorm effective approaches to solve the problem. The solutions proposed should be based on what they can do or change rather than what others can do or change. For example, if a student is feeling disrespected by their peer, they can choose to calmly express their feelings, set a firm boundary, or walk away.

You can also show students how to categorize solutions into tiers to inform the best decisions to make. First-tier solutions could respond to everyday social challenges like being interrupted while speaking. Second-tier solutions could respond to boundary violations like being called hurtful names. Third-tier solutions could respond to serious social offenses like bullying, property destruction, and physical abuse.

After you have taught and reinforced problem-solving skills, provide opportunities in the classroom for students to practice them. Some of the ways you can incorporate problem-solving skills in learning include

- role-playing scenarios

- encouraging group discussions

- using social scenarios in problem-solving activities

- engaging students in perspective-taking exercises

- promoting self-advocacy through teaching life skills

Remember to make activities or lessons around social problem-solving skills engaging and inclusive of all students' learning styles and preferences. Offer praise and recognition to students who actively participate and demonstrate these skills in the classroom.

Checklist: Preparing College Applications

There isn't a lot of hand-holding that occurs in high school—however, one specific area in which your students will need your guidance is preparing for life after high school. Deciding on the path to take after high school requires careful thought and planning. Students may need your help with conducting research, weighing their options, filling out applications, completing employment résumés, and developing the necessary skills for college or full-time employment.

Due to the challenges that students with ASD face at school, they may be hesitant about going to college and studying further. Fortunately, there are special needs programs administered in some colleges that can help to make the transition smoother. But with that said, going the college route may not be suitable for every student. Get into the habit of discussing life after high school with your students to help them start planning early and discover their unique interests and passions.

Below is a checklist you can use to guide students who are preparing their college applications. Note that you can also create checklists and schedules for other after-school tasks such as setting up a career profile on LinkedIn, creating a résumé, and creating a business plan.

Junior summer: Weigh your options

Set up a professional email address.

Complete an online psychometric

assessment.

Create a list of pros and cons for potential colleges you would like to attend.

Visit the college websites and take note of the application deadlines.

Find out about admissions tests and exams and set goals to start preparing for them.

Junior year: Schedule and take admissions tests and exams

Take admissions tests and other recommended tests (e.g., AP and IB exams) as required by your desired colleges.

Retake admissions tests and exams, if possible, to improve your test scores.

Senior year: Get your applications ready

Read the guidelines for filling out your college applications. Refer to the FAQs or call the school if you have any questions.

Complete your college applications and prepare other documents as supporting evidence (e.g., formal résumé, recommendation letters, and motivation letters).

Have two people proofread your applications and supporting documents before submitting them.

Submit college applications and save copies of your applications and supporting documents on your computer.

Complete financial aid forms, if necessary.

Pay application fees, if necessary.

Request applicable transcripts and reports to be sent to the colleges.

Check your emails regularly for correspondence from the admissions office.

Receive a confirmation letter from the admissions office.

Receive a financial aid award letter, if applicable.

Decide which college offer you are going to accept.

Follow the next steps given by your chosen college.

High school comes with added pressure and demands which can take a toll on students with ASD, especially when they haven't grasped critical executive function skills. To help them manage the responsibilities that come with high school, you can modify your teaching practices to enhance your students' strengths.

We have now completed the fourth part of the book, which focuses on specific ASD strategies to adopt at different education levels. We can now proceed to the conclusion, which provides a summary of what you have learned throughout the chapters.

Conclusion

To measure the success of our societies, we should examine how well those with different abilities, including persons with autism, are integrated as full and valued members.
–Ban Ki-Moon

Enhancing the Classroom Environment Begins With You

It is becoming increasingly common for children to be diagnosed with autism. This means that there could be some students in your classroom who are diagnosed (or are yet to be diagnosed) with ASD. Several years ago, it was only expected for special education teachers to learn about disabilities like autism, since they would be the ones who interact with such students regularly. However, more students with disabilities are being accepted into mainstream schools, which means that regular teachers need to know how to engage with and support students on the spectrum.

Adapting your style of teaching requires you to understand your students' needs and implement diverse and inclusive strategies to make sure that all students, regardless of their academic needs, feel confident participating in the classroom. Furthermore, since ASD is a spectrum disorder that affects students to different degrees, your challenge as an educator is to create a multidimensional learning experience that considers various sensory needs, learning styles, and social preferences.

Without a teacher, a classroom loses its vibrancy and foundation. Your dedication to learning more about ASD and how it affects students can create a supportive environment where students feel like valued members of the class despite the unique challenges they may face. This can increase their level of engagement, promote positive peer relationships, and allow them to develop a sense of competence and confidence in who they are.

The objective of this comprehensive teacher's guide was to present ASD in a manner that you may not have seen before. You were taken on a journey inside the minds of students in your classroom so that you could see firsthand how living with autism affects the way someone learns and interacts with others.

Throughout the book, you have been shown different strategies to address ASD-related behaviors like sensory overload, meltdowns, social anxiety, inattention, and so much more. What separates these strategies from normal classroom strategies is that they are tailored to support autistic and provide a multisensory experience for them. The advantage of incorporating these strategies into your instruction and teaching practices is that you can accommodate students' different learning needs and styles and ensure that learning materials are accessible to everyone.

Please note that while these strategies are effective in managing ASD in the classroom, some students may require individualized support to succeed socially and academically. Keep your journal near you and monitor students' behaviors to identify challenging behaviors early and take the necessary steps to address them. Be open to collaborating with parents and other support staff in tackling core issues affecting students.

The Path of Continuous Learning

To stay on top of your game and up-to-date with the latest models and methods for instructing students with ASD, continue to invest in your personal and professional development. There is so much that you can learn about yourself and your profession by reflecting on your classroom practices and setting meaningful goals to improve the learning experience. The group and individual activities mentioned in Parts 1–3 have been designed to help you further your growth and development beyond reading this book.

You have what it takes to transform your classroom into a space where learning feels inspiring, friendships are built, and students desire to become the best versions of themselves. Start making positive changes today and watch as your students flourish right before your eyes!

If this book has been valuable in helping you become a better teacher, leave a review and comment on the Amazon page, and help other teachers locate this resource!

About the Author

Richard Bass is a well-established author with extensive knowledge and background on children's disabilities. Richard has also experienced first-hand many children and teens who deal with depression and anxiety. He enjoys researching techniques and ideas to better serve students, as well as guiding parents on how to understand and lead their children to success.

Richard wants to share his experience, research, and practices through his writing, as it has proven successful for many parents and students.

Richard feels there is a need for parents and others around the child to fully understand the disability or the mental health of the child. He hopes that with his writing people will be more understanding of children going through these issues.

Richard Bass has been in education for over a decade and holds a bachelor's and master's degree in education as well as several certifications including Special Education K-12, and Educational Administration.

Whenever Richard is not working, reading, or writing he likes to travel with his family to learn about different cultures as well as get ideas from all around about the upbringing of children especially those with disabilities. Richard also researches and learns about different educational systems around the world.

Richard participates in several online groups where parents, educators, doctors, and psychologist share their success with children with disabilities. Richard is in the process of growing a Facebook group where further discussion about his books and techniques could take place. Apart from online groups, he has also attended training regarding the upbringing of students with disabilities and has also led training in this area.

A Message from the Author

If you enjoyed the book and are interested on further updates or just a place to share your thoughts with other readers or myself, please join my Facebook group by scanning below!

If you would be interested on receiving a FREE Planner for kids PDF version, by signing up you will also receive exclusive notifications to when new content is released and will be able to receive it at a promotional price. Scan below to sign up!

Scan below to check out my content on You Tube and learn more about Neurodiversity!

References

Admin. (2022, February 22). *Teaching children about reading social cues.*
    Soul Shoppe.
    https://soulshoppe.org/blog/2022/02/22/teaching-
    children-about-reading-social-cues/

Aided communication. (n.d.). AAC Community.
    https://aaccommunity.net/ccc/aided-communication/

Alisha. (2022, March 29). *How receptive language builds the way to successful
    communication for children with autism.* Healis Autism Centre.
    https://www.healisautism.com/post/receptive-language-
    builds-way-successful-communication-children-autism

Asaro–Saddler, K. (2013, January 1). *Improving the written expression of
    children with ASD.* Autism Spectrum News.
    https://autismspectrumnews.org/improving-the-written-
    expression-of-children-with-asd/

The Autism Community in Action. (n.d.). *Social skills.*
    https://tacanow.org/family-resources/social-skills/

Autism Specialty Group. (2021, September 15). *Autism sensory issues:
    what to look for & how to help.*
    https://www.autismspecialtygroup.com/blog/autism-
    sensory-issues

Bauers, D. C. (2014, July 15). *How to help your autistic child adjust to
    middle school.* LinkedIn.
    https://www.linkedin.com/pulse/20140715025943-
    26176682-how-to-help-your-autistic-child-adjust-to-middle-
    school/

Bennie, M. (2018, March 19). *Executive function: what is it, and how do we
    support it in those with autism? Part I.* Autism Awareness Centre
    Inc. https://autismawarenesscentre.com/executive-function-

what-is-it-and-how-do-we-support-it-in-those-with-autism-part-i/

Bennie, M. (2020a, February 23). *Teaching the concept of time.* Autism Awareness Centre Inc. https://autismawarenesscentre.com/teaching-the-concept-of-time/

Bennie, M. (2020b, June 14). *Calming strategies to support an autistic person.* Autism Awareness Centre Inc. https://autismawarenesscentre.com/calming-strategies-to-support-a-person-with-autism/

Bennie, M. (2023, February 1). *Collaboration in education—working together for positive outcomes.* Autism Awareness Centre Inc. https://autismawarenesscentre.com/collaboration-in-education-working-together-for-positive-outcomes/

BigFuture College Board. (n.d.). *College application checklist.* https://bigfuture.collegeboard.org/plan-for-college/apply-to-college/application-process/college-application-checklist

Boryga, A. (2023, September 22). *12 ways to help students identify their emotions.* Edutopia. https://www.edutopia.org/article/12-ways-to-help-students-identify-their-emotions/

Building social skills: Initiating play and making friends. (n.d.). Everyday Speech. https://everydayspeech.com/blog-posts/no-prep-social-skills-sel-activity/building-social-skills-initiating-play-and-making-friends/

Butler, A., & Ostrosky, M. M. (2018, September). *Reducing challenging behaviors during transitions: strategies for early childhood educators to share with parents.* National Association for the Education of Young Children. https://www.naeyc.org/resources/pubs/yc/sep2018/reducing-challenging-behaviors-during-transitions

Center for Development and Disability. (2019). Visual supports for children with ASD. In *Center for Development and Disability.*

https://cdd.health.unm.edu/autismportal/wp-content/uploads/2019/10/Visual-Supports-for-Children-with-ASD.pdf

Centers for Disease Control and Prevention. (n.d.-a). *Screening and diagnosis of autism spectrum disorder.* https://www.cdc.gov/ncbddd/autism/screening.html

Centers for Disease Control and Prevention. (n.d.-b). *Signs and symptoms of autism spectrum disorder.* https://www.cdc.gov/ncbddd/autism/signs.html

The Challenging Behaviour Foundation. (2021). *Information sheet— Positive behaviour support planning: Part 3.* https://www.challengingbehaviour.org.uk/wp-content/uploads/2021/02/003-Positive-Behaviour-Support-Planning-Part-3.pdf

Children's Hospital of Philadelphia. (2020, June 9). *Diagnostic criteria for autism spectrum disorder in the DSM-5.* https://www.research.chop.edu/car-autism-roadmap/diagnostic-criteria-for-autism-spectrum-disorder-in-the-dsm-5

Conditions that can occur with autism. (2022, October 26). Raising Children Network. https://raisingchildren.net.au/autism/learning about-autism/about-autism/conditions-that-occur-with-asd

Contreras, N. (2023, March 23). *How to write an effective IEP.* NWEA. https://www.nwea.org/blog/2023/how-to-write-an-effective-iep/

Cooke, S.-E. (2021a, July 14). *How to create a sensory-friendly classroom.* Sensory Friendly Solutions. https://www.sensoryfriendly.net/how-to-create-a-sensory-friendly-classroom/

Cooke, S.-E. (2021b, August 14). *What is a sensory-friendly environment?* Sensory Friendly Solutions.

https://www.sensoryfriendly.net/what-is-a-sensory-friendly-environment/

D, R. (2021, November 27). *Speech and language difficulties faced by autistic children*. Wellness Hub. https://www.mywellnesshub.in/blog/speech-and-language-difficulties-faced-by-autistic-children/

Davis, H. (2021, February 18). *Sensory overload in autism*. The Carmen B. Pingree Autism Center of Learning. https://carmenbpingree.com/blog/sensory-overload-in-autism/

Davis, K. (2012). *What triggers anxiety for an individual with ASD?* Indiana Resource Center for Autism. https://www.iidc.indiana.edu/irca/articles/what-triggers-anxiety-for-an-individual-with-asd.html

Deolinda, A. R. (2021, March 23). Understanding and utilizing the TEACCH method. *Autism Parenting Magazine*. https://www.autismparentingmagazine.com/asd-teacch-method-works/

Deolinda, A. R. (2023, September 25). Autism reading comprehension: Tips and teaching strategies. *Autism Parenting Magazine*. https://www.autismparentingmagazine.com/autism-reading-comprehension/

Devine, A. (2024, January 25). *Personal space—how to teach the concept to children*. Teach Early Years. https://www.teachearlyyears.com/a-unique-child/view/sen-space-invaders

Diament, M. (2022, December 2). *"Autistic" or "person with autism"? It depends*. Disability Scoop. https://www.disabilityscoop.com/2022/12/02/autistic-or-person-with-autism-it-depends/30154/

Emma. (2021, January 6). *Autistic body language*. NeuroClastic.
https://neuroclastic.com/autistic-body-language/

Eredics, N. (n.d.). *9 ways to teach social skills in your classroom*. Reading
Rockets. https://www.readingrockets.org/topics/social-
emotional-learning/articles/9-ways-teach-social-skills-your-
classroom

Friedman, A. J. Quote. (n.d.). In *Inspirational autism quotes,* (n.d.). Atlas
Foundation for Autism.
https://www.atlasforautism.org/quotes/

Gordon, B. (2007, April 2). *Speech and language problems in ASD*.
Kennedy Krieger Institute.
https://www.kennedykrieger.org/stories/interactive-autism-
network-ian/speech_and_language_problems

Grandin, T. Quote. In Emily, (2024, April 30). *Quotes about autism:
spreading awareness, understanding, and acceptance through powerful
messages*. Parent Press. https://getgoally.com/blog/20-
quotes-about-autism-that-we-love/

Hamstead, B. H. (2024, February 5). *Fostering inclusive classrooms for
diverse learners*. LinkedIn.
https://www.linkedin.com/pulse/fostering-inclusive-
classrooms-diverse-learners-hebert-hamstead-tdwdc/

Hardwick, L. Quote. In Emily, (2024, April 30). *Quotes about autism:
spreading awareness, understanding, and acceptance through powerful
messages*. Parent Press. https://getgoally.com/blog/20-
quotes-about-autism-that-we-love/

Hathaway, A. (n.d.). *Flexible seating for the classroom - OT & kid approved*.
Develop Learn Grow.
https://developlearngrow.com/flexible-seating-in-the-
classroom/

Healthdirect Australia. (n.d.). *Speech development in children*.
https://www.healthdirect.gov.au/speech-development-in-
children

Hendrickx, S. (n.d.). Quote. In *80 autism quotes to inspire and educate*, (2023, October 11). Apex ABA. https://www.apexaba.com/blog/autism-quotes

Higgins-Walsh, E. (2023, January 27). *What is augmentative and alternative communication and how can it benefit autistic people?* National Autistic Society. https://www.autism.org.uk/advice-and-guidance/professional-practice/aug-alt-comm

Hobbs, K. G. (2023, August 21). The benefits of visual supports for children with autism. *Autism Parenting Magazine.* https://www.autismparentingmagazine.com/benefits-of-autism-visual-supports/

Hoffman, M. (n.d.). *What are the types of autism spectrum disorders?* WebMD. https://www.webmd.com/brain/autism/autism-spectrum-disorders

Hollander, E., & Burchi, E. (2018, March 26). *Anxiety in autism spectrum disorder.* Anxiety & Depression Association of America. https://adaa.org/learn-from-us/from-the-experts/blog-posts/consumer/anxiety-autism-spectrum-disorder

How do visual supports help autistic students? (n.d.). Jade Autism. https://www.jadeautism.com/how-do-visual-supports-help-autistic-students

How to help your ASD child with their communication skills. (2021, January 6). Lumiere Children's Therapy. https://www.lumierechild.com/blog/how-to-help-your-asd-child-with-their-communication-skills/

Hume, K., & Indiana Resource Center for Autism. (n.d.-a). *"I can do it myself!" Using work systems to build independence in students on the autism spectrum.* Reading Rockets. https://www.readingrockets.org/topics/autism-spectrum-

disorder/articles/i-can-do-it-myself-using-work-systems-
build-independence

Hume, K., & Indiana Resource Center for Autism. (n.d.-b). *Structured
teaching strategies for students on the autism spectrum.* Reading
Rockets. https://www.readingrockets.org/topics/autism-
spectrum-disorder/articles/structured-teaching-strategies-
students-autism-spectrum

Individual education plans. (n.d.). Victoria.
https://www2.education.vic.gov.au/pal/individual-
education-plans-ieps/guidance/how-develop-individual-
education-plan

Kesherim, R. (2024, March 1). *Effective IEP goals for autism spectrum
disorder.* Total Care ABA.
https://www.totalcareaba.com/autism/iep-goals-for-autism

Larkey, S. (2019, September 9). *Using special interests to motivate and
engage students.* Sue Larkey. https://suelarkey.com.au/using-
special-interests/

Lee, A. M. I. (n.d.). *What is a functional behavioral assessment (FBA)?*
Understood.
https://www.understood.org/en/articles/functional-
assessment-what-it-is-and-how-it-works

Lee, A. M. I. (n.d.). *What is the Individual with Disabilities Education Act
(IDEA)?* Understood.
https://www.understood.org/en/articles/individuals-with-
disabilities-education-act-idea-what-you-need-to-know

Loftus, Y. (2023, October 2). Autism subtypes: Understanding the
spectrum. *Autism Parenting Magazine.*
https://www.autismparentingmagazine.com/understanding-
autism-subtypes/

Magro, K. (n.d.). Quote. In *80 autism quotes to inspire and educate,* (2023,
October 11). Apex ABA.
https://www.apexaba.com/blog/autism-quotes

McCann, L. (2020, March 17). *Autistic pupils and homework*. Reachout Autism Support Consultants. https://reachoutasc.com/autism-and-homework/

Milestones Autism Resources. (2019). *Homework tool kit*. https://www.milestones.org/files/assets/homework-tool-kit-printable-2019.pdf

Moller, R. (2023, October 16). *Teaching writing to students with autism*. Above & Beyond ABA Therapy. https://www.abtaba.com/blog/teaching-autism-students

Morphoses. (2023, November 30). *Mastering the clock: Fun and effective ways to teach kids time management*. LinkedIn. https://www.linkedin.com/pulse/mastering-clock-fun-effective-ways-teach-kids-time-management-c5q4f/

Morris, A. (n.d.-a). *Conversation social skills for listening*. The Watson Institute. https://www.thewatsoninstitute.org/resource/conversation-skills-listening-2/

Morris, A. (n.d.-b). *Social skills for asking for help*. The Watson Institute. https://www.thewatsoninstitute.org/resource/i-can-ask-for-help/

Moss, H. Quote. In Emily, (2024, April 30). *Quotes about autism: spreading awareness, understanding, and acceptance through powerful messages*. Parent Press. https://getgoally.com/blog/20-quotes-about-autism-that-we-love/

Multisensory learning in the classroom: A teacher's guide. (2021, December 2). Structural Learning. https://www.structural-learning.com/post/multisensory-learning-in-the-classroom-a-teachers-guide

National Autistic Society. (n.d.). *Anxiety*. https://www.autism.org.uk/advice-and-guidance/topics/mental-health/anxiety

National Autistic Society. (2020, August 21). *Visual supports.*
https://www.autism.org.uk/advice-and-guidance/topics/communication/communication-tools/visual-supports

Nikki. (2021, March 15). *Building relationships with students.* Teaching
Autism. https://teachingautism.co.uk/building-relationships-with-students/

Parker, H. (n.d.). *Individualized education programs (IEPs) for autism.*
WebMD.
https://www.webmd.com/brain/autism/individualized-education-programs-ieps-for-autism

Picture exchange communication systems (PECS). (n.d.). Kid Sense Child
Development Corporation.
https://childdevelopment.com.au/areas-of-concern/using-speech/picture-exchange-communication-systems-pecs/

Pierce, R. (2023, October 31). *Autism and transitions: 20 strategies to ease
changes in routine.* Life Skills Advocate.
https://lifeskillsadvocate.com/blog/autism-transitions-strategies-to-ease-changes-in-routine/

Practical strategies for teaching social problem-solving in high school. (n.d.).
Everyday Speech. https://everydayspeech.com/sel-implementation/practical-strategies-for-teaching social-problem-solving-in-high-school/

A quote by Adele Devine. (n.d.). Goodreads.
https://www.goodreads.com/quotes/1238916-children-with-autism-are-colourful---they-are-often-very

A quote by Alan Turing. (n.d.). Goodreads.
https://www.goodreads.com/quotes/6150884-sometimes-it-is-the-people-no-one-can-imagine-anything

A quote by Albert Einstein. (n.d.). Goodreads.
https://www.goodreads.com/quotes/8136665-everybody-is-a-genius-but-if-you-judge-a-fish

A quote by Ban Ki-moon. (n.d.). BrainyQuote.
    https://www.brainyquote.com/quotes/ban_kimoon_64372
    2

A quote by Charles R. Swindoll. (n.d.). BrainyQuote.
    https://www.brainyquote.com/quotes/charles_r_swindoll_
    388332

A quote by Max de Pree. (n.d.). BrainyQuote.
    https://www.brainyquote.com/quotes/max_de_pree_12575
    6

A quote by O. Ivar Lovaas. (n.d.). Goodreads.
    https://www.goodreads.com/quotes/456840-if-they-can-t-
    learn-the-way-we-teach-we-teach

A quote by Rosemary Crossley. (n.d.). Goodreads.
    https://www.goodreads.com/quotes/1334878-not-being-
    able-to-speak-is-not-the-same-as

Robson, D. (n.d.). *How to teach kids about personal space.* And next
    Comes L. https://www.andnextcomesl.com/2017/03/how-
    to-teach-kids-about-personal-space.html

Rudy, L. J. (2024, February 9). *5 reasons why an autism diagnosis is missed.*
    Verywell Health. https://www.verywellhealth.com/high-
    functioning-autism-260305

Schwartz, B. (2022, September 15). *Self-soothing: What it is, benefits, &*
    techniques to get started. Choosing Therapy.
    https://www.choosingtherapy.com/self-soothing/

Self-advocacy: children and teenagers with disability, autism or other additional
    needs. (2023, November 17). Raising Children Network.
    https://raisingchildren.net.au/autism/school-play-
    work/school/self-advocacy-children-teenagers-disability-
    autism

7 autism behavior and communication strategies. (n.d.). National University. https://www.nu.edu/blog/7-autism-behavior-and-communication-strategies/

7 calming strategies autism every parent or guardian should know. (2022, April 29). Daybreak Independent Services, Inc. https://www.daybreakis.org/news-stories/7-calming-strategies-for-autism-every-parent-or-guardian-should-know

Sharma, S. (2023, November 3). *How students can rethink problem solving.* Edutopia. https://www.edutopia.org/article/strengthening-high-school-students-problem-solving-skills/

Stanfield, J. (n.d.). *8 ways to encourage independence and self-advocacy for kids with autism.* James Stanfield. https://stanfield.com/8-ways-to-encourage-independence-and-self-advocacy-for-kids-with-autism/

Teaching strategies and classroom policies to help students with anxiety disorders. (2022, April 25). Teach.com. https://teach.com/resources/helping-students-with-anxiety-disorders/

Tortora, T. (n.d.). *How to strengthen executive functioning skills for autistic children.* Stages Learning. https://blog.stageslearning.com/blog/how-to-strengthen-executive-functioning-skills-for-children-with-autism

Unknown. (n.d.). Quote. In *80 autism quotes to inspire and educate,* (2023, October 11). Apex ABA. https://www.apexaba.com/blog/autism-quotes

Van Berkel, T. Quote. In Emily, (2024, April 30). *Quotes about autism: spreading awareness, understanding, and acceptance through powerful messages.* Parent Press. https://getgoally.com/blog/20-quotes-about-autism-that-we-love/

Vrana, C. (n.d.). *Leveraging special interests to help children with autism: An autistic person* shares her experiences.* Stages Learning. https://blog.stageslearning.com/blog/leveraging-special-interests-to-help-children-with-autism-an-autistic-person-shares-her-experiences

What does it mean to be "on the spectrum?" (2016, April 12). Milestones. https://advancingmilestones.com/news/what-does-it-mean-to-be-on-the-spectrum/

What is LAMP? (n.d.). Lamp Words for Life. https://lampwflapp.com/about

Zager, D., & Curiale-Feinman, S. (2013, January 1). Executive functioning enhancement for high school students with ASD. *Autism Spectrum News.* https://autismspectrumnews.org/executive-functioning-enhancement-for-high-school-students-with-asd/

Zauderer, S. (2023a, September 15). *Four functions of behavior in ABA therapy.* Cross River Therapy. https://www.crossrivertherapy.com/aba-therapists/four-functions-of-behavior

Zauderer, S. (2023b, September 20). *5 ways autism can affect learning.* Cross River Therapy. https://www.crossrivertherapy.com/autism/how-autism-affects-learning

Zauderer, S. (2024, January 21). *IEP goals for autism: How to set meaningful objectives for your child.* Cross River Therapy. https://www.crossrivertherapy.com/autism/iep-goals-for-autism

Zurcher–Long, E. Quote. In Aiyer, R. (2023, March 13). *51 inspirational autism quotes.* FirstCry Parenting. https://parenting.firstcry.com/articles/magazine-inspirational-autism-quotes/

Image References

Chernaya, K. (2021, June 29). *Kids doing artwork* [Image]. Pexels. https://www.pexels.com/photo/kids-doing-artwork-8535599/

Danilyuk, P. (2021a, June 21). *Boy in orange shirt playing train toy on the floor* [Image]. Pexels. https://www.pexels.com/photo/boy-in-orange-shirt-playing-train-toy-on-the-floor-8422249/

Danilyuk, P. (2021b, June 21). *Boys inside a classroom* [Image]. Pexels. https://www.pexels.com/photo/boys-inside-a-classroom-8423399/

Danilyuk, P. (2021c, June 21). *Kid writing on a notebook* [Image]. Pexels. https://www.pexels.com/photo/kid-writing-on-a-notebook-8423070/

Danilyuk, P. (2021d, June 21). *Student showing his drawings* [Image]. Pexels. https://www.pexels.com/photo/student-showing-his-drawings-8423048/

Holmes, K. (2020, November 17). *Crop ethnic schoolgirl with teacher during class* [Image]. Pexels. https://www.pexels.com/photo/crop-ethnic-schoolgirl-with-teacher-during-class-5905926/

Крамор, M. (2022, May 20). *A woman teaching a young man* [Image]. Pexels. https://www.pexels.com/photo/a-woman-teaching-a-young-man-12197305/

Krukau, Y. (2021a, June 4). *Group of students talking at a staircase* [Image]. Pexels. https://www.pexels.com/photo/group-of-students-talking-at-a-staircase-8199169/

Krukau, Y. (2021b, July 4). *Little girls and boys having fun playing with colorful balls* [Image]. Pexels. https://www.pexels.com/photo/little-girls-and-boys-having-fun-playing-with-colorful-balls-8613146/

Krukau, Y. (2021c, July 4). *Woman reading a book to the children* [Image]. Pexels. https://www.pexels.com/photo/woman-reading-a-book-to-the-children-8613089/

Krukau, Y. (2021d, July 5). *Children playing foosball* [Image]. Pexels. https://www.pexels.com/photo/children-playing-foosball-8617571/

Pak, G. (2021, May 20). *Photo of a group of friends sitting on the grass* [Image]. Pexels. https://www.pexels.com/photo/photo-of-a-group-of-friends-sitting-on-the-grass-7972671/

RDNE Stock Project. (2021a, February 24). *Boy sitting on his desk looking angry* [Image]. Pexels. https://www.pexels.com/photo/boy-sitting-on-his-desk-looking-angry-6936379/

RDNE Stock Project. (2021b, June 26). *Boy in blue polo shirt showing a book to a teacher* [Image]. Pexels. https://www.pexels.com/photo/boy-in-blue-polo-shirt-showing-a-book-to-a-teacher-8499549/

RDNE Stock Project. (2021c, June 26). *Woman in pink sleeveless shirt using black laptop* [Image]. Pexels. https://www.pexels.com/photo/woman-in-pink-sleeveless-shirt-using-black-laptop-8500303/

Thirdman. (2021a, July 27). *A teacher helping her student* [Image]. Pexels. https://www.pexels.com/photo/a-teacher-helping-her-student-8926900/

Thirdman. (2021b, July 27). *Students raising their hands inside the classroom* [Image]. Pexels. https://www.pexels.com/photo/students-raising-their-hands-inside-the-classroom-8926542/

Made in the USA
Columbia, SC
28 October 2024

45212939R00115